THINKING HARDER

For a complete list of Management Books 2000 titles
visit our web-site on http://www.mb2000.com

THINKING HARDER

Being Smart About Transformation

Duncan Bury
Jane Buick

2000

First published in 2010 by Management Books 2000 Ltd
Forge House, Limes Road
Kemble, Cirencester
Gloucestershire, GL7 6AD, UK
Tel: 0044 (0) 1285 771441
Fax: 0044 (0) 1285 771055
Email: info@mb2000.com
Web: www.mb2000.com

British Library Cataloguing in Publication Data is available

ISBN 9781852526429

Acknowledgements

Writing a book like this is not just the product of my mind. It is the distillation of ideas, thoughts and conversations I have had over a number of years. So on that basis I acknowledge anyone to whom I have spoken.

Of particular influence in my life has been Bob Lord, without whom my thinking would have remained conventional. He sadly died far too young and I think about him every week as I work with clients. A true friend, mentor and a great inspiration. His ability to challenge me to look at myself in a different way has stayed with me throughout my career.

I must acknowledge all those managers I have worked for, from my first proper job where the manager hired me because I used the word "eclectic" on my CV, something he said I should never have done, to my last CEO who told me my job role was to "stir the sh*t" in the organisation. Tragically I don't think he told anyone else, which made my job much harder. In between I should like to thank the manager who picked up a red pen ready to "correct" whenever I walked in his office with a piece of paper and the manager who replied to every one of my challenges with the phrase "Stop being defensive Duncan." I realised she used this as a destabilising tactic with everyone. To all those managers I thank them for the insights they have given me.

Colleagues who have inspired me include Angela Cleverly, who always complained that automotive components such as pistons and camshafts should come in a variety of colours and Tod Eby in Canada who proved that accountants can have a sense of humour and can really care.

Of course I need to acknowledge Jane Buick for giving me belief in myself and my sometimes crazy thoughts and also for getting me to say what I mean in words other people can understand – even if she calls me "Rain Man".

My thanks go to William and Sean, whose moments of support and laughter during our evolution has exceeded one day easily and provided the most embarrassing moment of my life that I will never share with anyone, but it was a lesson learnt.

I also acknowledge all my children, Sophie, Tom, Lucy and Laura, and my step-children, Jed and Max, who have been a rich area of research in human behaviour on a daily basis. Not forgetting the dogs, Phoebe aka "Ugly Dog" and Jasper aka "Chief", who are looking forward to long walks again now that the book is finished.

Lastly, to my parents... My mother who has read this from beginning to end and thinks it's a bit new-fangled (thanks, Shakespeare, for that word), and my late father who told me to take risks, even though he never did himself and considered brown shoes with a blue suit very bohemian.

To them all I acknowledge their input, not least the advice about risk. I suppose this book is part of taking a risk or two.

Duncan Bury

It is a strange thing, writing your first book, albeit jointly. It causes you to think about your subject much harder than you ever have done previously. It also opens up an opportunity to say thank you to a number of people. In sitting down to write these acknowledgements I realise that the people I write about and the support they have given ripples further than I can imagine because without so many of them I would not be here now, nor would I have the confidence to set off on my next adventure, whatever that may be.

Firstly I must thank Deirdre Nuttall, who got this whole thing moving in the first place. Her patience was endless and for this we are grateful.

My thanks to all of our clients, many of whom we now consider friends. Our stories only exist because of the times that you created.

To my wonderful family which represents what feels like a modern day Waltons, with six amazing children, some more grown up than others. There are simply too many of you in this family to mention – suffice to say that if you have a regular dining chair at our house then I include you in the word "family". There have been more than the inevitable ups and downs over the last 18 months and at least one of you has always been there. Of course my mum needs a special mention, a bit like the queen in that respect but a lot more approachable when your brain has gone dead and you can't remember how to spell "once".

To my true friends who always asked "how is the book?" and hovered around long enough to hear my rants. Sarah and Louise especially as they were usually at the end of a phone line trying to work out what on earth this book was all about and at the same time did a great job of sounding interested.

To a special man, Mr George Hay, a history teacher and a source of much inspiration. He instilled in me enough self-belief to get me this far. I hope this somehow convinces you that running the debating society at Preston Lodge High School was worthwhile.

To another special man, my partner in every sense, Duncan. My best friend who has reinforced the lessons learnt from Mr Hay and continues to kick, push and pull me forwards always saying "of course you can" on a daily basis.

Finally to my dad who is no longer in this world but whom I am fairly convinced has kept watch as writing continued into the wee small hours and if looking in now will be delighted this has come to an end so that his daughter's language may now return to that of a lady.

Jane Buick

Contents

Introduction

Five years ago we set out on a mission. To find out why most change initiatives failed to deliver what was expected of them. That is what people have told us and what we have observed. Something happens but not necessarily what was predicted. Not in the financial sense, as we know that the balance sheets of companies can tell stories. The term "creative accounting" did not come from nowhere, nor did the phrase "accounting for growth". Not in a technical sense either, as we know that things can get done on time, on budget and to specification if you push people hard enough and throw enough resource at it. Software implementations can be forced through. New machinery can be installed; new "ways of working" can be documented and become part of governance procedures.

No, we wanted to know why when the "change" had been "completed" people still talked about the old world, the way things had been. We never saw anyone advocating the return of tooth extraction without anaesthetic or walking ten miles to market for fresh produce. No, they were of course referring to the world they were aligned to, not how things had literally been at the beginning of time. We wanted to examine how organisations tackled change initiatives and the methodologies they were using. We wanted to know why the people aspects of the change were in the main considered to be poorly done.

There wasn't one organisation that we looked at where the staff considered the leaders in the organisation had got "change" right consistently. We heard the same phrases over and over again. "They never think about us." "We do not know who is leading this." "Why do they never ask us what we think?" "The management are faceless." "Why don't they make a decision?" "If they say they are going to do it why don't they just do it?" "Our old systems worked but they changed them anyway." "No-one ever thinks about the impact on us." "I wonder if the CEO has kids and a partner to think about." "They aren't worried about their mortgage." "It's a job, I just wait for the change to go away and wait for the next announcement." And my personal favourite: "Change I love it. I exist in change, I am change..........I usually have my lunch at 12. Will we be done by then?"

There are, of course, a number of ways we could have tackled this. The most usual technique is the survey approach.

"How well do you think blah blah blah on a scale of 1 to 10 blah blah blah?"

This wasn't for us. We wanted to get involved in the change initiatives and explore for ourselves in a socio-anthropological sense what was going on. In 2004 we set up a company in the UK to offer change and transformation services to blue chip companies using a methodology that had evolved over our careers by seeing how not to do things. This wasn't like a "Rogue Change Agents Gotcha" approach we genuinely wanted to help organisations tackle transformation. One of my old colleagues gave me a huge insight as a new graduate. He said "Every situation can be learnt from. Even when people are telling you that *this* is the way to do something you may actually be learning that it is exactly not the way to do something. Those with insight learn to distinguish and store the knowledge." To balance this Zen-like coaching he also told me, "*'Tomatoes are a fruit'* is knowledge; not putting them in a fruit salad is wisdom."

A great example from our past, before our enlightenment, was a project where we were trying to *force* French Canadians to use a European French version of a software manufacturing resource system that we were implementing across the whole organisation. What the hell was their problem? Just get on with it! French is French right? Another example was being *told* to sell *more* pharmaceutical products into a saturated market place, full of competitors all selling the same product.

We did of course truly want to run a business helping companies get through change and our efforts were professionally motivated to help organisations progress. During the years we were working in this way, we also saw lots and lots of great "stuff" for which we try to give credit throughout this book. We also met many wonderful people who had the insight to laugh with us at some of the absurdities of their organisations. We also know that we rattled a lot of cages but rest assured that was never for any other reason than to get people to think harder. We may have got you naked, but you always left with your clothes back on.

We have worked across most conceivable sectors in many different departments. We have been shouted at, threatened and on one occasion accused of almost giving a very senior manager a coronary. He was our client and he has had us back since. In the end we left every intervention with at least a smile and a handshake but more commonly a mutual round of applause. It is indeed quite sad as we sit writing this book together, reflecting on the anecdotes, that as of 1st January 2010 we are no longer out there delivering transformation but instead are educating companies in how to do it themselves.

It's a tough world out there selling *thinking harder*. "What?" was commonly the response "We think hard already." Within an hour of working with people we demonstrate what we mean. The macho managers who can "go all day" are mentally fatigued by three in the afternoon and like any muscle their brains are straining to keep up with the effort of truly thinking harder. Only once has someone left and missed their station as they fell asleep on the train home. We always give a health warning though. You will be tired. Take care.

If you have ever facilitated a group of people you will know that you have to think on many levels. You have to think what is going on, how you are going to record it and respond to it and what you are going to do next. In our world we also had to do something else when we met people. We reframed our meeting into something powerful. We considered it field research for this book. Our priority was always to deliver great outcomes for the client but we always reflected on how the organisation worked, how they handled people, what were the cultural norms, what were the drivers for change, and what methodologies they were relying on and how they reacted to challenge. This reflection was normally achieved with a glass of Merlot in a bar or hotel after any meeting. We were outsiders, given the unique opportunity to look at organisations as if we were looking for the first time. We observed the minutiae of the organisation. We observed the culture, the language and the behaviours. We looked at relationships and norms. We were so enthralled by what we found that we became even more passionate about supporting organisations through transformation.

It is now five years on and we have finally found the time to sit down and write this book. Well we had time just like everyone else who was hit by the recession of 2008/2009. What was I saying about creative accounting? This book is not the story of the journey we went on, that's for another book, but this is a summation of working with companies and observing them. From the simple observations – *Dress down day on a Friday to show your individualism meant all the blokes wore chinos and a blue shirt and all the women wore black* – to the deeply disturbing – *You could say anything you wanted in meetings if you prefaced it with "building on that" and no-one would challenge you.* We saw bullying, cultural and social blindness, support, kindness, anger, hatred, respect and awe. We met people in roles they wanted and people in roles they didn't. We saw leaders and followers and not necessarily in those roles. We saw happiness and sadness and we saw success and failure. But most of all we saw people. People with context and lives. People with passions and dreams. People who wanted to succeed. The organisational cultures we observed were varied. Hierarchical and flat. Formal and informal. Directive and innovative. But we found that they all had one thing in common. They confused "change" with "transformation". They used the terms interchangeable without defining the meanings. They used "transform" frequently in the boardroom but it was attenuated to "change" by the time it got to the "shop floor". They talked a lot about how vital it was to keep people engaged, but then instantly disengaged them with directives, targets, acronyms and lack of decisions. They confused governance with reality and communication with telling. The management career tenure was about a tenth of the employee tenure. The managers looked ill informed on the history of the organisation. What was often new to them had been seen by staff before. And what they didn't know they tended not to care about. They talked engagement but measured delivery regardless of engagement. And they were all people.

I suppose one of our biggest frustrations was coming across the "Learning and Development" careerists whose role we considered should be more accurately defined as "Ignorance and Retardation." Organisational Development often fell into this category where the development of the organisation and individuals was limited to what the OD specialists knew or could grasp rather than what the organisation or individual could know or grasp. There were pockets of resistance to this stereotyping, but they struggled to turn the super-tanker with nothing more than a hand held fan. Whilst the generally highly educated managers and leaders in the organisation were crying out for intellectual models that actually delivered something, they were being offered traditional "Development" courses such as "Presentation skills", "Communication skills" or "Report writing skills", and being analysed against fixed criteria that determined whether they were a plant, a hamster or a red banana. All these development approaches operated at the behavioural level not at the thinking level, and in the organisations we observed all the individuals within them were thinking and capable of thinking some more. It's harsh, I know, but the amount of gate-keeping we found in organisations was immense. "Plan the work and work the plan" is a good maxim, but do you keep drilling holes by hand when someone offers you an electric drill? You do if you are in OD. When we found ourselves speaking with the CEOs of organisations or the Board Members they were enthused by what we were saying. We spoke of educating not training. We spoke of changing thinking not changing behaviours and they were enthralled. We spoke of engaging people not inundating them with governance and process.

The managers and leaders within the organisations we observed and spoke to generally considered the "OD" or "L&D" people to be delivering what they thought was required rather than what the leaders and managers required, and what's more, they moved at a snail's pace extending any development or intervention opportunity to fill the time available to them, not the client. To this extent they operated as gate-keepers and they grossly inhibited the organisations by fiercely protecting their positions as arbiters of what was right. It was a bit like the PC software operating system debate. Control the offering along with the market place so that people think there is no alternative. Managers and leaders constantly looked for ways to work around the procurement processes to find what they needed rather than what they were supposed to need. And when they were discovered they had their knuckles rapped, for doing what was required!

We termed this back-door approach "management by stealth". I always remember my first introduction to this technique as a young graduate as we purchased a kettle for our laboratory and got it through our accounts procedure by calling it an "ebullition device". It sounded very scientific and they never checked. But you can't do science without tea. Right?

We are not advocating breaking every rule. What we advocate is taking the corporate filters off. Looking at your world with fresh eyes. Seeing things as if you are from the planet Zog and acting on what you see.

We didn't set out to criticise what was going on out in the big wide world; we set out to see if we could interpret the actions that were being taken in order to transform organisations. It was like looking in on a lost village and trying to work out the societal rules from the actions we saw. What we found was that organisations were still using old change models, staff were still not engaged and leaders were still ignoring the emotional aspects of management. Fundamentally, thinking and emotions are what drive us, but the focus is on *behaviours.* People were obsessed with behaviours not thinking, and when we spoke of challenging thinking we often had that fed back as "you just want them to do something different as quickly as possible – like change their behaviours." Arghh!

One of the biggest insights we got from our work was that to transform organisations you had to become the epitome of what you were trying to achieve on a broader sense. If you wanted to be a listening organisation, begin by listening yourself. If you wanted people to share ideas, share your ideas. If you hated reading big reports, stop writing big reports. If you complain about meeting duration and frequency, then deal with the ones you own. We all have a choice. If you want the organisation to smile, you smile, if you want your colleagues to be supportive support your colleagues. Transformation so often starts with you and the choices you make.

So put on your chinos, your blue shirt or your black outfit, and, "building on that" let's begin the book........

1

React, Reframe, Align, Embed

There are many things that science does not yet know. We are living in an age where knowledge is exploding, however fundamental truths are more and more elusive. The haystack is getting bigger as our knowledge grows, but this makes finding the needles all the more hard. In 1820 Hans Christian Ørsted noticed the link between electricity and magnetism as a current through a wire deflected a close by compass needle. Faraday extended this and developed a unified theory of electricity and magnetism. To date, physicists have been able to merge electromagnetism and the weak nuclear force (may the force be with you) into the so-called electroweak force, and work is being done to merge the electroweak force and quantum chromodynamics into a QCD-electroweak interaction sometimes called the electrostrong force. I am told that there is also speculation that it may be possible to merge gravity with the other three into a theory of everything.

Our work has led us to believe that we have developed something like a theory of everything for managing people through transformation, and that is where we start.

As mentioned in the introduction, much of the content in this book is the result of experiences gained through our work as Miascape with many different organisations in diverse sectors. However when working with them, transformation was our job and it had to happen regardless of who they were and what the organisation did. The methodology had to be totally adaptable to the environment in which it found itself. In this chapter we hope to introduce you to that methodology so that, in our journey through the rest of this book, we may speak a language that we all understand.

Understanding what is going on in our minds is key to thinking harder, so we are going to start by understanding our own $E=mc^2$. As Einstein said: "Make things as simple as possible but not simpler." We have thought long and hard about how to best distil our methodology for transformation. Our own $E=mc^2$ is, we hope, as simple as possible but not simpler.

Models should have resonance and meaning. They have to have breadth and depth. The best models are demonstrably widely applicable and develop a life of their own as people begin to understand the deeper insights associated with them. Our $E=mc^2$ has demonstrated these characteristics and now we are sharing them with you.

Whenever change happens, the person it has happened to is sent on a journey towards a different future than the one that they originally envisioned. This journey begins with a reaction to the circumstances that have just presented themselves. On a small scale, most of us go through such an experience at least once most days.

There are many available futures and the path that takes us to our future is littered with decision points, impacts and considerations. There are no signposts pointing out "Joe Blogs, you are here and your future is here," although most of us would welcome such signs. We do not live in a linear world where one thing happens after another. Neither do we live in a constant size world where every input to our brain has the same level of importance. We are all constantly managing a myriad of "things" in order to move forward. The complexity is huge. If we take ten linear decisions with ten potential options for each decision point regardless of the previous decision we end up with 10000000000 possible futures. Who said that life is not complex?

To simplify things, let's take one instance of a situation we might find ourselves in to explore what may happen to our thinking during a sudden, unexpected change. Imagine you're eating a piece of toast all covered in jam. Something distracts you – a text arriving on your phone, the cat scratching at the window and asking to be let in or some more bad news on the radio about the global financial crisis. You turn too quickly, and you drop your toast. Of course, statistically, it has a fifty-fifty chance of landing jam-side-down but experience has shown you that, of course, it is going to land jam-side-down on the dusty floor. It was your last slice of bread. You had been doing a fantastic job of ignoring the fact it was past time the floor was mopped, but now the evidence is staring you in the face, firmly fixed to a copious amount of strawberry jam.

For a moment, you feel like screaming. But you don't.

"Oh well," you think. "I'll have cornflakes instead." You wipe the jam up off the floor, and then go and pour yourself a bowl of cornflakes, eat them and get on with your day. You promise yourself you'll clean the rest of the floor later.

What just happened? When something unexpected occurred in the course of eating breakfast, you instinctively reacted. Your reaction was dictated by the context you found yourself in: last slice of bread, milk and cornflakes in the cupboard, dirty floor. Maybe you even cursed out loud. Then, however, you started to reframe. You probably thought, "Oh well," and you itemised the things you needed to do to get your breakfast back on track (clean the floor, get some cornflakes instead). You quickly aligned with your new set of circumstances when you sat down to eat your bowl of cornflakes and pretty soon the whole experience had been embedded and you were just getting on with your breakfast as if nothing had happened at all. The reaction to the toast falling incident had passed and you were aligned to a different series of actions.

We refer to the process of getting back on track as "reframing". In reframing, we generally resort to our experience of the world in order to find an answer to the question of what to do. If our car is rammed, we think about all the things we know we need to do: call the insurance company, get the other driver's details, call the mechanic, organise alternative transportation. We know that all these things are important because of our experience with cars and transport. If our child falls ill and we have a deadline looming at work, we use our experience to run through the options available: call granny, work from home for a morning, plead ignominiously for a deadline extension, and so forth. *The difficulties in transformation occur when our existing strategies for reframing situations do not provide insightful solutions to problems.*

So where do these strategies come from? Well, we have all written a virtual book on psychology that we carry with us everywhere. Without it, we could not interpret the world. Based on this virtual book and our continued experiences of the world, we develop strategies for dealing with things intuitively. If we are really lucky, we gain access to the advice collected in the virtual books constructed from others' experience and interaction. Often these strategies are only valid insofar as they worked for the person who used them before, but we adopt them anyway. We also assume that everyone else's virtual book looks just like ours, with the same chapter headings, same indexing and the same or similar content.

We couldn't be more wrong!

It is not surprising that, when people share their virtual books with us, it is often hard to believe what we are seeing. Our assumptions about them and theirs about us have often been wrong. Our context is suddenly laid bare.

So what can we do? Let's look at a simple situation to try and understand the importance of the React, Reframe, Align, Embed approach.

Whenever anything happens, at home, at work, out shopping or on holiday – whatever the situation – we all go through the same journey of react, reframe, align and embed so long as we are allowed to go through this transformational process uninterrupted. Finding the process a little stressful at the beginning is perfectly normal and to be expected; the important thing is recognising that reaction, even painful reaction, is a healthy, ordinary, normal element of the journey. An example that we may identify with is the death of a loved one. This inevitably happens to everyone, but each time the grief is just as new and real and devastating as it was before. In the early stages of grief, it will be awfully difficult to talk about what has just happened. For weeks, or even months, we will be tearful and feel lonely and bereft whenever we think about the person who is gone. Gradually, so long as we are allowed to grieve properly, we will learn to accept what has happened. The day will come when we will be able to remember the good times with joy, and the grief will no longer be raw and immediate.

In the business environment, it is far from unheard-of for companies to announce major change abruptly, and then expect everyone to get on board with the minimum of complaint. Anyone who reacts strongly and negatively runs the risk of being characterised as a trouble-maker. Anyone who reacts strongly and positively may be seen as a "yes" person, a brown-nose, and can be seen as trying to score points within the team. The thing is, though, that reacting isn't just normal, it's an essential element of the process, and by insisting that an organisation's members repress or ignore their feelings when confronted with change, managers are setting the scene for disorder, ill-feeling and a failure to achieve transformation.

Let's assume, for the sake of argument, that Acme Internet Company has made a tactical decision to relocate most of its operations from London to a remote village in the Outer Hebrides. We'll take it as read that the EU has offered tax breaks and a sweetener to anyone willing to bring a high-tech industry to the isolated location. The locals are delighted; think of the boost to the Hebridean construction industry! This is good news, too, for local pubs and restaurants and for the school, which was suffering from depleted numbers. But this will also represent enormous change to the hundreds of workers who are now being asked to leave their comfortable pads in Chelsea and Notting Hill and move to an area that most of them have never even visited before.

While a few of the workers down in accounts are rumoured to be happy about the move – they are reputed to be an odd lot, obsessed by Star Wars and known to haunt the karaoke bar down the street – wild reports about the Hebrides have been circulating, including the worrying notion that sun-dried tomatoes and porcini mushrooms may not be available. And then there are all the practical dilemmas. Many staff have small children in school or Montessori, spouses or partners who work in London too, elderly parents around the corner, and established social networks and circles of friends. On hundreds of individual levels, there's a lot to react to, and people certainly are reacting. Management announces that they want to know who's on board by the end of the week, and that's about it. People are told that the Hebrides are fantastic; one of Britain's most beautiful spots, with loads to see, and enviably affordable real estate: "You're going to love it. You'll never look back! Once you get there, you'll see what we mean. The board sees this as the best opportunity you are ever going to have for a better lifestyle. Get on board! The Hebridean train is leaving the station and we all need to be on it. If you snooze you lose. *Let's go!"*

Nobody listens. "How do they know this is the best opportunity I'll ever have?" they think. Despite the rumours about the strange chaps in accounts who are definitely expressing enthusiasm for the change ("I bet they know something we don't about the transformation"), nobody feels the way they are being told they should. Nobody feels free to broach the subject openly in case they give too much away about their position or even their personal context. There's a general feeling that they've all been left in the dark for way too long, that accounts must have been involved in the decision, and that management has been assumptive if not downright disrespectful, but there is no open forum for talking things over.

In short, it's a right bloody mess.

Often, when an organisation has to undergo significant change and transformation, much will be said about employee "resistance" to the move. Resistance will be seen as something that has to be overcome, beaten out, worn down, eliminated, as if the employees' reactions were a wall to be broached and destroyed. This attitude does not exactly foster the sort of relationship between staff and management that helps the company to go forward. It underestimates the power and validity of the emotional response, and indicates to employees that the organisation actually doesn't really care about them, no matter what the managers say.

We don't like the word "resistance". In fact, we wouldn't be using it at all if it wasn't to pour scorn on the very notion. There's no such thing as resistance; there is reaction.

While we do encounter hurt, confused, upset, angry people in the face of decisions that are going to wreak change on every level, we don't consider this to be resistance. It is reaction. People who are enthusiastic or embracing the decisions that will wreak effort are not "yes people", they are also reacting. We see the responses to change, negative or positive, as normal, healthy reaction and we embrace it. By doing so – by accepting that we have started a process that should not be interrupted, because it is normal and healthy and appropriate – we can start to move beyond reaction and towards reframing.

The worst thing Acme's management team can do now is get truculent with those employees who aren't leaping on board. Angry staff, upset staff and even tearful staff are all reacting in perfectly normal and healthy ways to what is, after all, going to be a huge change in their personal circumstances. People who are genuinely positive about the changes are also reacting in a perfectly normal and healthy way. In each case, employees' personal context determines their reaction. Some will have to wrench themselves away from established lives, and some will, inevitably, have to decide that it is time to leave the organisation and move on. Some will already be calculating the risk associated with taking "the package" and becoming self-employed, something they have been promising themselves for years. So that the company can continue to do well, however, it is important for them to permit and facilitate the process of reframing. This won't be the same for everyone.

When we encounter angry, negative people, we feel just as positive about the outcome of change as when we encounter positive people. Why? Because to be either negative or positive, it is necessary to expend a huge amount of energy, and energy provides the impetus to create lasting change. Real apathy is more worrying as little can be done without energy of some description.

When the initial panic at Acme Internet subsides, some will start to think, "OK, I was thinking of leaving this job anyway – I've learned all I can here. This is a good opportunity to move into another area..." and others might think, "The Hebrides, eh? Well, this will be an opportunity to reduce my carbon footprint; I'll be able to install a wind generator on the roof of the house." Some might even think: "I've been dragging my feet about dumping my boyfriend for way too long. This will be the perfect excuse! He can't follow me to the Hebrides."

Everyone will have to go through their own personal reframing process, whether that means leaving the organisation, continuing in a changed role, or staying in the same role in a very different location. The specifics of how Acme's employees react will depend on their context at home, at work, in their relationship with their colleagues and managers, and in terms of their own mental landscape. People who are ready for a change anyway will find it easier to embrace their new set of circumstances; those who have created fulfilling lives in London that they are loath to leave behind will find a way to disengage from the organisation. Those who don't really care either way – well, it's probably time for a change for them anyway.

In order to help people to effect meaningful change in the way they approach life and work, we find that it is important to go way beyond small, incremental changes. As we mentioned, we all look to our past experience for inspiration as to how to reframe. For important change, we need to learn how to set aside this instinctive response and, having exhausted our already acquired strategies, find new ones.

Creative insightful reframing happens when existing thinking strategies are exhausted and issues are considered from new perspectives.

Reaching out to find new solutions makes it possible for us to reframe successfully.

As the reframing process is undergone, it has a ripple effect. As each person creates a new reality for themselves from their new set of circumstances, their changing situation impacts on all those around them.

At Acme Internet, it's an exciting environment to be in:

"Half the people from accounts have decided to take the redundancy package and stay put," says Olive. "That means that if I go to the Hebrides, I'll be in a more senior position. I don't like sun-dried tomatoes anyway. I'm ready to go!"

"I've been offered a redundancy package," says Sid. "I was really annoyed at first, but it's enough money for me to go and stay in an Ashram in Mumbai for a year, which I have been wanting to do for a while now, so I think it's maybe a blessing in disguise. Next stop, enlightenment!"

"I've been offered a promotion and a raise," says Hector. "I'm going to miss London a lot but this is a great opportunity for me and a few years away from the rat race won't hurt. Life is cheaper, too, so my wife will be able to take a career break for a couple of years and take care of the triplets."

What's going on? People are, in their own way and in their own time, aligning to their new life circumstances. They are getting used to the idea of change. They are undergoing a process of transformation. They are in a very real sense in a new world in which much has changed.

In any organisation, management can make it more probable that people go through transformation effectively by fostering, rather than inhibiting, people's natural, instinctive responses to change. How? By allowing people to react, whatever the reaction, rather than insisting that everyone pay lip-service to the idea that the change is a good one, and by creating an environment in which people can reframe creatively, intelligently and with the emotional and practical support of the organisation. These are all big things that need to be handled sensitively and smartly.

For a new employee coming on board after a successful transformation has happened, however, there is little sense of the upheaval that has occurred. A new reality has been created. For those who are with Acme in the Hebrides, their decision to move has already become part of who and what they are. If they have been allowed to pass through the four stages of transformation, they will not feel that they have to strive constantly to return the world to where it was before the incident.

In our company, we directors laughed uproariously when one new employee submitted a holiday request form for nine months ahead. He had no idea how, during the long, difficult months after starting our own business, holidays were non-existent, and we thought twenty-four hours a day about the business and its potential for survival. He could not imagine how exhilarated we were when our first customer bought our services. Now, our employees also exist in the new world that has been created, and they have no knowledge of our previous context.

Transformation can be challenging and it can be difficult but it is never impossible. Crises pass. The chaos does not last forever. The complexity changes. The miners' strike of the 1980s, the poll tax of the 1990s in the UK, Vietnam, the Opium Wars, the aircraft hijackings of the 1970s, the unemployment after the Second World War, Nelson Mandela's incarceration on Robyn Island; it does all pass and make way for something new. Our world is not still reacting to the Black Plague or the Roman Empire forging into Europe. Others' transformations are not necessarily ours and we are not aware of the emotional turmoil our predecessors went through to create the current world. We simply exist in it.

When problems do occur when change is being attempted, it is usually because something has happened that has not allowed the members of an organisation to traverse the normal sequence of events and emerge on the other side. In the case of Acme, while some of the employees reframed successfully on their own, others found it difficult, and were given little or no support. Some of them moved to the Hebrides, but they weren't very happy about it and now people are sitting in their shiny new offices looking glumly out at the rain and saying, "This isn't like it was in

London. In London, we did things differently. All the computers were lined up on the other side of the wall, and the secretaries didn't grab all the biscuits at coffee-time, the way they do here..." and "I miss Joe from accounts. Things wouldn't be like this if he was still here. Remember Joe? He used to do the books differently, with that other software program. I liked that program. I wonder what Joe is doing now." You can imagine how effectively these people are working at the moment.

Things aren't helped by Natasha, the new supervisor, cheerleading for the new circumstances every day by giving pep talks about how everyone has to "put their heads down and deal with things as there's nothing we can do about it anyway" and chattering on about the freshness of the sea air. They all hate Natasha with a passion. At the same time, several of Acme's key programmers decided to stay in London, despite the fact that the organisation valued them so much, and despite the fact that they had no real reason not to come. Not having been given the chance to process their reaction, they just didn't see a way through the way they felt, and could only resort to choosing a response from their anterior experiences. "I have been here before. I felt uncomfortable. Last time I got a new job. It worked. I will do it again."

These feelings of bereavement, loss, anger and a score of other negative sentiments cannot be railroaded away. Being enthusiastic about the change has to be managed as well. Management cannot insist on change or eliminate these feelings with round-robin emails or heavy-handedness or a lot of cheery talk about "making it happen". We all need to respect that reaction is normal and healthy and proper. The nature of the reaction depends on the context of each individual person. We can and will come through it to accomplish meaningful transformation. People can be taken on a journey of transformation, but they will never reach the destination if they are prodded all the way. As your grandmother may have taught you, you can take a horse to water, but you can't make it drink.

In organisations that respect the thinking harder process, people are culturally, attitudinally and strategically aligned and all of this means that there is fertile ground for lasting change – for change to be embedded, for transformation to occur. When this happens, the electrifying, unbeatable energy bound up in those profound emotional responses can be transferred to other areas of life including, of course, work.

In order to really understand this process, it's not necessary to look to the corporate world. Think about it. We can all see people reacting, reframing, aligning and embedding every day. If you consider this, you'll be able to recognise this process in yourself too and the wonderful thing about understanding the process is that it stops being scary or stressful. You will be able to start to think: "OK, I'm just reacting to this. I know that I will begin to reframe this situation shortly and I will come out of this thing. I'm angry/elated about this just now, but in ten minutes I'll be back to normal."

We have done some work with a financial institution which found that despite profits rising as a result of employees efforts, the employees were not engaged with the organisation, and that they were getting less engaged all the time. The management, which had a relatively high turnover with managers rotating every three years or so, had no idea what was going on.

In working with the employees, it quickly emerged that people weren't reacting to things occurring in their workplace *now*, but to a change that had happened fifteen years ago! Management had no idea, because none of the current managers had even been on the scene all that time ago, and did not understand the context of the staff. Several of the managers had still been in school. The staff, however, were still talking about, "Do you remember how it used to operate fifteen years ago?" The reason why they still needed to talk about these things was simply that they had never had a chance to be listened to. They had never been allowed to react, reframe, align and embed. Instead, they were characterised as negative, inflexible and difficult and just *resisting* the latest, greatest idea.

Has anybody ever said to you, "I'm going to tell you something but I don't want you to react," or "I'm going to tell you something, but don't be angry"? When people say such things to us we say, "Don't tell us that, because you can't tell me I'm not allowed to react. I need to be able to react." The reaction (!) we get to that response is usually consternation and an impulse to carry on telling us anyway.

Often, organisations say, "We're going to change but you're not allowed to react to it. You've just got to get on with it." Or "We're going to restructure and it's going to be fantastic. You are going to love it."

Excuse me? Listen to what the employees are saying: "You can't tell me to love it because you don't know my context!" People are getting cross and agitated and upset before they've even had time to think about what is going on and what it will really mean for them.

Unfortunately, in the real world, most organisations don't do things in the right order and they don't understand the importance of the emotional element to change and transformation. What we have learned is that all the energy and excitement that is created in the process of doing something can be taken and used in a positive, useful way.

Emotion is key. Ask people how they *feel* about something, and they will usually be able to talk for hours. Ask them what they are going to *do*, and the conversation will probably be over in minutes. By harnessing the energy bound up in emotion and linking it directly to actions, great things can be achieved.

And that, my friends, is the "thinking harder" way.

2

The Genesis of Thinking Harder

In the following pages we would like to give you some insight as to why, we believe, thinking harder is so important and how it may be adopted easily by anyone interested in this approach.

The world is a complex place. The numbers involved in this complexity rapidly become too large to really handle. Let's think about having a cup of coffee in Glasgow. That's where I am right now. A quick search on my iPhone tells me there are 260 cafes in the City Centre. Each one may offer six different types of coffee so we are now at 1560 possible cups of coffee I could drink, but we are not finished. Even just take-away or stay-in adds another layer of complexity 3120. Sugar or not sugar. We are at 6240. Milk or not milk? Skimmed or full milk. Porcelain or Paper cup. Extra shot or not. OK so I'll have a skinny latte with no sugar in a proper cup in the Millennium Hotel by Queen Street Station. Oh bugger I forgot to factor in hotels that sell coffee. So let's say we are at a complexity number now of say 10,000. Now I have to get to the location. Do I walk or catch a cab? Which route do I take? Do I park the car for 1 hour or 2 hours? Will it rain or not rain? Did I bring a coat or not? When we start thinking about the world we live in and the decisions we have to make we realise pretty quickly that if we actually contemplated every option in what we were about to do we would never move from the spot we are in. As an experiment just monitor which foot you set off walking with when you start from scratch. I bet you have never even noticed which is your dominant foot. When you start monitoring it you will slow down; make decisions and add time to what you intended doing. Suddenly the complexity of what is *actually* in your world impacts you. I know it's not *that* relevant but it is an example of how we filter things out in order for us to cope with the complexity of the day. We all background subtract. We are programmed to stop feeling, hearing, or seeing things once they become part of our quasi-stationary state. We stop hearing the ticking clock, we stop smelling our perfume, we stop noticing the train passing the office window.

We stop noticing the things that make up our sensory world until they change. We are brilliant at detecting change and we are brilliant at re-focusing when our brain is stimulated. If a cat is exposed to a continuous click it responds to it, but after a while it becomes normal and there is evidence that the auditory nerve no longer even sends information to the brain. As soon at the ticking stops however the cat takes notice. It is an amazing phenomenon in humans we get through life by filtering stimuli out, but instantly notice them if they change. So you know your house has a smell all of its own. Do you know what it is? Next time you walk in try to be alert to the sensory onslaught that others pick up.

So in order to deal with our world we filter things out. We become stressed when we cannot filter things out and they impact us. The problem is we don't all use the same filters. And that is where the problems really start. In fact we can become so focused on what we are doing we filter out really impactful big stuff. There was a famous experiment where people were asked to count the passes in a basketball match. In the middle of the action a person in a gorilla suit walked on court. The majority of people in the experiment didn't even see it, well perhaps their eyes saw it but something filtered the information so it never reached consciousness.

Whilst working in Corporate life I realised over a period of time that everyone carries with them their version of a complex world that has been attenuated to allow them to cope with it. When people come together they often assume that their attenuated world fits neatly into every other attenuated world they meet. Like a jigsaw coming together. My experience of this, of course, is that it is not true. However, leaders in organisations continually assume, in our experience, that if they push hard enough the attenuated worlds will suddenly merge together as if they were a giant jigsaw just waiting to be completed. Keeping the jigsaw metaphor alive, imagine we are all part of one huge jigsaw, each of us being a piece. The chances of two individuals in a population of 60 million bumping into each other and finding that their pieces fit together is pretty slim, about 1 in 15 million actually, assuming each piece has 4 adjacent pieces! You have more chance of winning the lottery. So the point of all this is that the attenuated world people carry with them is their *context*. The genesis of "thinking harder" began when I realised that the context in which people find themselves determines their interaction and reaction to the world around them. So remember from this point forward that CONTEXT is important. As an experiment write down a list of phrases describing the place where you are reading this book. You will probably get bored pretty quickly describing where you are, and you will satisfy yourself at some level that you have described the situation well. Now ask a colleague in the same room to do the same thing. Compare the lists. Similar. Dissimilar. My guess is that the lists and the detail will be different. When asked to describe any situation we find ourselves in we describe our attenuated version until we begin to THINK HARDER and at that point we start describing the reality of the complex environment we find ourselves in. This is when we really start engaging.

The "thinking harder" approach began formulating when I

realised that we live in an attenuated world – but everyone's is different.

The more I thought about this concept of attenuated worlds the more I realised that the standard change and transformation approaches I had experienced were wrong. Wow, that's a bold statement to make. But really, every single change model I had ever come across reinforced the thesis that people *resisted* change. It was a natural state to be in, apparently. Change was proposed and people resisted it. This is not the whole story. The insight I had was that people *reacted* to change dependent upon their *context*. In fact I would go further than this and say that people *react* to anything dependent upon their context.

So transformation and change within organisations is not challenged by resistance it is challenged by reaction. Now try finding that in a book on change. OK so it's in this one, I'll give you that.

Humans are unique and similar at the same time. What a contradiction. We all have roughly two legs and two arms, one head, two ears two eyes, etc., etc. However the one brain we have enables us to develop a uniqueness in thought that enables us to perceive the world in a certain way. We are all wired differently. I am not colour-blind, I know, I have done the tests, but I have a real issue with red and green at traffic lights. I will sometimes stop at green and sometimes begin to go on red. No matter how I try, I cannot overcome this. I will share more of the crazy things people have to put up with if they know me. I get confuzzled with "g" and "j", so much so that I have to say "guh" and "juh" to distinguish them like a primary school child. I also struggle with the ends of words differ-ent or differ-ant appar-ent or appar-ant. No matter how hard I have tried over the years I cannot "remember" the correct endings. I am not stupid. I am just wired differently.

I became aware that other people are wired differently too.

Sometimes the wiring is established and sometimes the wiring is emerging. I use this analogy all the time to explain why teenagers display such strange behaviours. They have not yet finished the wiring loom. So what does this have to do with the genesis of *Thinking Harder*. Well I realised, again simple when you say it out loud, that people perceive things differently, hear things differently, use language differently, and behave differently depending upon how they are wired. Until you establish norms between the individuals there is no guarantee that you will make any progress in transformation. If you do not establish the norms then you are interpreting, but interpreting with your context!

Making things happen begins by exploring the simple stuff first. What do you mean by "think"? What is "success"? What is "failure"? What is "no time"? What is a "framework document"? What is a "proposal"? What is "work"?

I always ask a client how they would like to receive a proposal. They often look astounded. "Would you like an MP3, a picture, a cartoon, a document?" However, until they explain I have no idea what is in their head associated with the word "proposal". Just to be clear, no-one has ever said "on one knee holding roses and an engagement ring".

Our worlds are unique, the way we use language is flexible and what we hear, see and smell is influenced by our wiring.

Language is incredibly simple and incredibly complex in the same moment. "I love you" is a simple phrase full of complex meaning, and "set" a simple word with more meanings in the English language than any other word. Set the table, set the jelly, one set to love, belong to that set, etc. I realised that simplistically we assume we communicate meaning and understanding when we use words to communicate. That assumption can be dangerous unless we are all familiar with the implied meaning. I once went to South Africa to work as a young graduate. I asked a colleague if they would help me fill in a form, they replied "I'll do it just now." I stood for the best part of half an hour outside their office before asking again when they would help me. They again replied, "I'll do it just now." "What does that actually mean?" I asked. "I'll do it in a while," they replied. When a South African uses "just now" substitute "later" and you will be fine. Another example closer to my home is my Glaswegian friends who are in the habit of saying "I'll see you after" as you leave. "After what?" I used to ask. They looked at me blankly "After you've left," they replied. The phrase should be (I am guessing): "I'll see you again after you have left this time." My favourite sign recently was in Glasgow. It was in the window of a Herbalist Shop. It said quite intimidatingly: "We specialise in all kinds of pain." Language, simple but complex.

So what did all this tell me. Firstly, having a common language when working on transformation projects is essential. The language of transformation we call it. Other activities have it. Computer programmers speak their own (ever more complex) language using words like inheritance, polymorphism, object, iteration, but they understand each other. Accountants use PBIT, EBIT, credit, debit, gross, net, input tax, output tax. Mathematicians use fractal, complex, within the limits, attractor, and each knows what it means. As Richard Feynman the great physicist said, a bird is a bird is a bird before it was called bird, Ousieu, Pájaro or Vogel by anyone. Transformation is a nebulous thing, though, and has no intrinsic definition. It is nothing until someone defines it. It is not an object waiting to be named. It is a descriptor not an extant thing. It has to be defined in a way that a bird does not.

Floccinaucinihilipilification is an English word but unless I tell you what it means, assuming you don't know, you have no understanding of it. It means the act of estimating as worthless. It is not used much now but an example is provided by Sir Walter Scott.

"They must be taken with an air of contempt, a floccinaucinihilipilification of all that can gratify the outward man." (Sir Walter Scott, *Journal*)

Words are shapes on a page and mean nothing until they are defined. This is the reason why shouting a word at foreigners does not help them understand it better. We have to use language we all understand to describe the complexity of things we don't understand. This is a purpose of this book, to define a language of change, a language of thinking harder and a language of transformation.

I tell a true story, because I was there, of a man and woman in a bakery in Menorca, one of the Iberian Islands off the coast of Spain. The woman said to her husband, the man, "You ask for the bread because you speak the lingo better than I do." The man stepped forward and said in a strong Yorkshire accent, in loud English I might add, "I want two..." shaking his first and second digits in a v form at the shopkeeper, a common vulgar gesture around Europe, "...baguettes," using his thumb and first finger moving up and down as if sliding down a pole to project the shape of a baguette – an even more vulgar gesture in Europe. His communication failed with him being asked to apologise prior to someone who was bilingual stepping in to clear up the misunderstanding.

My insight here was that clearly words have no intrinsic definition. If you use language you must define what you are saying in some common way.

Definitions are interesting and they change. The word "nice" is a good example in the English language. In the late thirteenth century it meant "foolish, stupid and senseless". In 1400s it meant "dainty" or "delicate". In the 1500s it meant "precise and careful". In 1700s it became "kind" or "thoughtful" and by the 1900s it had become a vague word meaning "acceptable" or "pretty".

What about the word "gay"? That has changed its meaning also and its usage. Words also contract their meaning and become more specific. One example being the English word "cattle". Once any animal was called "cattle" from the French word "Catel" meaning property, that eventually became the English word chattel meaning personal belonging. Words are interesting, dynamic and variable. Unless we define what a word means it has no meaning! This book is full of the obvious isn't it? So why is this relevant to us when we are talking about thinking harder about change?

Well, what exactly does "change" mean and what exactly does "transformation" mean? I used to hear these words used interchangeably and I began to think that there was a difference. When I questioned people on their definitions I often got the response that there was no difference, they were interchangeable. The genesis of *Thinking Harder* became more real when I determined that there was a distinction between change and transformation. This is what I came up with. Change can be purposefully or randomly reversed. Transformation is irreversible. Think of baking a cake. I can put the ingredients on a table and move them about and then leave the room. Someone can purposefully or randomly put the ingredients back to where they used to be. That is change. If we bake the cake, we cannot go back to where we were. That is transformation. *Thinking Harder* is about transforming individuals, teams and organisations so that the future world becomes the norm and no-one thinks about the ingredients they are too busy eating the cake.

We all react to comments made by others to us, in either a positive or a negative way – actually, sometimes it can be a neutral response too. The degree of the reaction is related to how much we value the opinion of the person making the comments to us. I realised some time ago that this was a distinction I was not making when someone made a statement to me. "How much do I value this individuals opinions?" I was treating each comment made, by different people, with the same weighting, implying that I valued the opinion of the individual to the same degree.

This might seem like an obvious insight, but If I can use one example... Driving down the road I inadvertently pulled out in front of another vehicle (it must have been a red light!). I instantly recognised I had made an error and held my hand up to apologise. The other driver ignored my apology and began a silent (well, we can never hear the other person, can we?) but animated assault on me. I could have reacted in the same vein, shouting abuse, gesticulating and flashing my lights. This would have got my adrenaline running and affected my driving ability for the next few minutes. Instead I asked myself the question "given I have never met this person, let alone spoken to them, how much do I value their opinion of me?" The answer of course was I didn't. Therefore I left the scene relaxed and comfortable in the knowledge that I had not wasted any of my energy beans on them.

Thinker Harder began when I realised that I didn't need to value everyone's opinions in the same way. I should learn to ask the question about "value" before I reacted.

Organisations document tons of things. The governance processes are beginning to dictate more and more how the organisations run. I quickly recognised in organisations that the written rules of the organisation were there to refer back to in the event of transgression by individuals. What really ran organisations were the *unwritten* rules. It is the same in any "relationship". Whilst we may be explicit about some rules ("love and obey, for richer for poorer", etc.) the actual day-to-day rules, which are often not verbalised, define how we interact on a day-to-day basis. "I'll clean the car and you cook the tea," for example, may emerge as an unwritten rule in our family. It is these rules that can constrain our thinking and dominate our behaviour. It may get to the point where it would never cross our minds to suddenly clean the car. "Do you fancy trying a new position tonight, darling?" "OK, you do the ironing and I'll sit on the sofa watching football."

The combination of written rules and unwritten rules can be used to determine the mental models of the individual and the organisation. Let's think of an example. When my old CEO came into the room the conversation always turned to golf as he loved the game and would always have time to speak about it. Unwritten rule: "if you want to engage with the CEO talk about golf." So what does this tell us about our beliefs? 1) The CEO always wants to talk about golf and 2) We make best use of our time with the CEO by talking about golf not the business.

Other unwritten rules in organisations abound. The "boss" always sits in the power position at meetings, the centre top of a horse shoe table. Casual day means chinos and a blue shirt for men and black anything for women. Meetings must be at least half an hour long because that's what our scheduling package says. The MD gets a parking space by the door and the machine operator parks far, far away because the MD can't get wet coming in to work but the machine operator can.

Examining these unwritten rules allows us to understand how organisations really run. And it's not pretty.

Unfortunately I quickly found that telling organisations how they really operated was a bit like telling a mother her baby is ugly. They react badly. We had to devise a way to get organisations to SEE the issues for themselves. It is not enough to *tell* them about the inefficiencies, inconsistencies, unacceptable behaviours, lack of vision and poor strategy; they have to *see* the truth for themselves to get them in a place to transform. This was the first challenge of thinking harder. How to show people the reality of the situation without making them feel bad and at the same time showing them that to transform anything they had to transform their thinking not their behaviours.

Here we stumbled upon *cognitive dissonance*. Cognitive dissonance is the discomfort we feel when our actions and beliefs are not aligned. More of this later. Suffice to say at this early stage, even when your actions and beliefs don't match you are likely to come up with all sorts of reasons why what you do is acceptable even when you don't believe it. It's amazing, isn't it? We meet lots of people who know smoking is bad for them but still do it. Why? Well, they can always find a reason. "I'll stop next week." "I need it to keep calm." "It's my only pleasure." "I am only young I'll stop when I am older." Now if the smoking story is an easy target what about "ethical shopping"? Do you think people should be exploited to make cheap products for our market place? I suspect you don't. Do you buy clothes from high street retailers? The chances are you are buying products that have been provided unethically. How does that feel?

The last insight before I launched into *Thinking Harder* was that you had to make things more probable to happen than not. What does that mean? Well, put simply, of the 10,000,000 outcomes that are possible we want to make it more probable that the outcome we want happens. How do we do this? By working with people to make it more probable. Think of trying to get someone off a diving board. You can carry them up and throw them off once you have decided they have to go. This is not the best way. Do you see the analogy here of the Boardroom decision and the "just do it" approach?

Making it more probable they will go of their own accord is harder. Taking them to the bottom of the steps is not good enough. Taking them up the steps is not good enough. Taking them to the end of the board is not good enough. You have to tip the board on which they are standing so that they lean forward, lose balance and it is more probable at that point that they will dive off. A simple analogy. Put a ball on a flat table and it will stay where it is. Lift the table and it will roll randomly. Carve a path in the table and lift the table and it is more probable that the ball will end up where you want it. Let's go right back to the beginning now. Telling people to change their behaviours is like lifting the table. Changing thinking is like getting them to make the groove and lift the table themselves.

3

Never Mind the Change Curves

Yes, for those of you who have ever sat in a lecture theatre and tried desperately to pin your eyes open long enough to copy down into a grubby note book this model of change and that theory of organisational development, overshadowed of course by your lecturer's own personal favourite, the Kubler Ross change curve, I apologise to you for the following pain.

Since the dawn of time, clever humans have enjoyed making models, both physical models (boats, buildings, planes) and abstract models to describes how something is supposed to happen.

I, on the other hand, and others like me I am sure, have lived in wonder and occasional bewilderment at the natural world. A single cell and a few others like it, made from molecules of this and that, made from atoms and bits, all stack up, differentiate a bit, and bang you have a human!

I know it's not that simple and this is a very crude approximation of the anatomy and physiology which goes together to make a human being. It really is a wondrous thing which even entire text books struggle to cover in any depth, and a model is impossible on a transactional level.

As a result of admiring the complexity of humans I have a developed a resistance to over-simplistic models, and in particular change curves. If you can't put in a text book what it is to *be* human, then trying to extract what happens to thousands of humans, their emotions and behaviours when their organisation decides to do something differently into a linear curve on a page is just plain dumb!

As I write this we are browsing the internet for current "change models". They all have stuff in common and stuff which is different but do they really tell us anything about change, or, as we prefer, *transformation* in organisations?

My considered and restrained response on this is that they may be useful in getting an idea across but that's it. Beyond that the simplicity ends as you enter into the real world of personalities, egos, phobias and experiences and things become complex.

However, I realise that sometimes a picture is good. It's a start and we can go on from there to explain how these lines on a page relate to reality. So in the interests of this I present below *React, Reframe, Align, Embed* in model form. Pretty simple. Now I am trusting you not to go beating people around the head with this one and if you are by any chance a lecturer in a business school please take your poor students to the pub instead and draw this for them on a beer mat when it comes to the lecture on change.

REFRAME	*ALIGN*
REACT	*EMBED*

"Ah, so you are just the same as everyone else then," I hear you gasp! No, and here comes my timely defence.

You will note that we talk of "React" rather than a specific behaviour or emotion because all behaviours and emotions are possible depending on the contexts of the individuals. We then talk about "Reframe". We discuss the fact that people will start to think about things. We don't say how they will think or what they come up with; how could we second guess that? We *will* say that the *React* and *Reframe* phases will require the greatest amount of time, effort and resource.

"Align" is all we say about the fact that at some point it all needs to start coming together. We don't say how, but we do say that if the first two phases are addressed then this will take proportionately less time and resource. Finally, we have "Embed" and we talk about what this may look like in reality towards the end of this book.

If I had to say what I felt was most important about this model it would have to be the fact that it is recursive, something which is difficult to show on a linear model but we will have a go below.

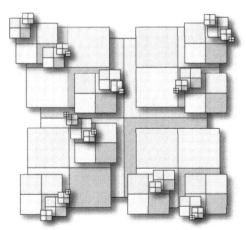

Recursion of React Reframe Align Embed

The fact that this model is recursive means that you can drop down an infinite number of times into any phase of the model and recreate the model in full before popping back up to the levels again to where you started. It is also fractal in that it works at the World level, the Country level, the City level, the Town level, the Organisational level, the Department level, the Team level and the Personal level. It is scale independent.

This recursion is important in organisational transformation because no transformation is truly linear and the impact scales both up, down and across the organisation. There is usually great complexity and interdependency. Things just don't happen in a step-by-step fashion.

When we are problem-solving, we generally know how close we are to the solution. If I ask you to build a model aircraft you can tell me roughly where you are in solving it on a scale of 1 to 10. If I give you a string of numbers to multiply, again you can tell me roughly where you are on a scale of 1 to 10 in solving it. In transformation we need to explore *insight*. With insight you never know how close you are to solving the challenge. Generally you exist in 1, then leap to 10 as the "Aha" moment happens. Interestingly you can explain insight solutions to others just like a problem solution, making the two processes similar. Supporting people through transformation is supporting them through problem-solving – that is, putting in governance, introducing technology, etc., but more often than not it is about supporting them through insight.

Our model is based on a sequence of events, but there is no start or finish or "getting on" point. Everyone will join this transformation model at a different place and it is the role of the transformation architect to manage the complexity of the transformation activity.

So there we have it, The Miascape transformation model. This is not about problem solving but insight. We hope you gain it.

4

The World Is Back to Front

How do you begin transformation and where do you start? Well the answer is not easy. The standard business school models seem to propose that an organisation team or individual operate in discrete linear activities that can be isolated, halted, redesigned and implemented. You begin at THE START and finish at THE END. The truth of the matter is much more complex than that. At any one time an individual – and in fact the organisation – is handling an enormous amount of complexity. Each activity in which you are involved is at a different stage of development and in the context of our approach people will be reacting to demands, reframing their ideas and strategies, aligning their colleagues, friends clients and suppliers or embedding the transformation for each of the different activities in which they are involved. Just thinking about the activities I am involved with right now I can come up with:

- Writing this book
- Organising our first off-site art exhibition
- Developing our accreditation course with Edinburgh Business School
- Buying a new house
- Selling a house in France
- One of our children is applying to University and does not know what to do

- We are looking at growing the company in 2010
- Preparing for Christmas
- And the Lurcher-cross-Scottish-Deerhound dog we call Phoebe but everyone else seems to call "Ugly Dog" has just chewed through the PlayStation Controller Cable – again!

What is your list of activities or plans you are involved in? Maybe you should make a list right now and look at the interactions of them all. My guess is you will be in a different place with each activity. Your life is only linear in time, but not in activities. Your life is multidimensional and current change models try to simplify this to be understandable. But they are insufficient to deal with that complexity. Plus they do not take into account those around you and their transformation journeys. These people are all moving through reacting, reframing, aligning and embedding.

People you interact with are going through that same process and the people they are interacting with are doing the same. It is an infinite chain of interactions in multi-dimensional space. Your activity, like the flap of the butterfly's wings in chaos theory causing a hurricane, generates reactions in others. Right now we are about to give notice to our landlords as we move into a house after two years of dithering about buying a house. Somewhere there is someone who will be moving into this house BECAUSE we have left it. They just don't know it yet.

When we interact with people, their reactions are of course related to their emotional relationship to the context. More emotion means more reaction. Telling you we are moving house probably did not create any huge emotional reaction. However my mother on the other hand, not one to hold back, said she was "glad we were buying a house as she was losing sleep over us renting for so long".

So essentially we are all on a number of transformation journeys. Not just one. They are all at different positions in time and should we decide to adopt the "thinking harder" approach we have to ask ourselves at which point do we begin. The answer is of course NOW. It doesn't matter where you are in the transformation process of any particular activity; we can determine that once we are involved. But jump in now. Do not wait for things to start faltering or running out of control before getting involved. Do not see the transformation in a linear fashion. Begin the transformation approach now. Educate yourself in the transformation approach and pretty soon you will see that you can recognise where people are, where the project is, where the stakeholders are and what needs to be done to move things forward. You can begin to label the stages of transformation and begin to recognise the multi-dimensional nature of transformation and its impact on others.

Get involved now using a transformational approach is the message, but more often than not such an approach is only sought when things start to go wrong.

Here are a couple of examples. In one organisation we were asked to coach a senior individual who was having difficulty leading people through transformation. We were briefed by his line manager: *"We have given him six months to get this project started and engage people. He has failed. He has difficulty relating to people and will not listen to anyone else. You can have a go at this but I know you will fail."* What a place from which to start!

So this is what we heard from this initial conversation.

"We have given a member of staff a job to do but have not given him any training or support."

"We have waited six months before we do something about it."

"The rest of the staff have assumed he will fail because that is what we are telling people."

"There is nothing we can do to help and there is nothing you can do to help."

"He is too senior to need help."

The outcome of course was another fluke. We engaged with the individual and discovered he was struggling with the transformation. He was highly educated and his training dictated that his technical field gave him all the skills to deal with people as dealing with people is easy, apparently. However he quickly discovered that he had no idea how to tackle the transformation. He did recognise from his functional role that the culture in which he existed was "if you succeed you get no support, if you fail support is provided". Therefore the approach to most things in the organisation was plan to fail so that resources are provided retrospectively. He had waited six months until his line manager finally decided to do something about it. How back to front is that! But how unique is this? Not very. He recounted numerous stories from the organisation rewarded failing departments with more budget, more training and more personal development. Successful departments were rewarded with a reduction in budget and targets being increased. Bizarre.

Example two. Integration of two geographically dispersed organisations. One group were failing to engage. The management had *told* the group to integrate. They spent twelve months waiting for the group to integrate. Nothing changed. Communication broke down. People would not stay in the same room with their colleagues. Performance was affected. After twelve months it was time to throw some resource at the groups. What did we find? Yet again, the group did not know how to manage the integration. They were assumed to be capable. The management assumed it was their role to *tell* people what to do. The integrating teams had no respect for the internal support as they were educated to different *academic* levels in their respective disciplines. The intellectual capability of the transformation leaders was constantly being challenged by the group, whose members were beginning to enjoy their position of mavericks within the organisation.

With a transforming approach and by listening to each party we began to make progress. When we spoke to the same organisation twelve months before about this particular integration they told us that they had no issues with the integration, it was going to run fine. It was only when it went wrong that resources were found and time made available to get involved. The problem was at that point not only do you have to design the project; you have to *recover* the project as well. A huge mountain to climb instead of a ski-jump to a transformed organisation.

This issue is not unique, it is endemic. Organisations try to minimise current costs in transformation; they fail to *think harder* about the transformation they are attempting and then have to find out why failure happened and put it right. It is a real case of mountains out of molehills and organisations do this to themselves all the time.

The world is back to front, especially the world of work and business. No-one has the time to deal with an issue properly – that is, until something goes wrong. Let's explore this bold statement a little. I am often asked to work with groups to explore strategy, tactics, implementation and transformations. These projects are generally huge. They could run over three years or more. They may be related to building a new hospital, integrating services, university collaborations, moving factories or relocating services around the world. The tasks faced by individuals are great at the beginning, middle and end of the projects. The demands put on their time are great and they have limited availability. What they choose to do at any point is key. They can focus and deal with issues through *thinking harder* or they can superficially deal with things, make seemingly good decisions, based on their existing thinking strategies in a rapid fashion and hope that the outcome is what they desire. This is the quick-fire decision-making we see in films. Remember Gordon Gekko, the financier and corporate raider played by Michael Douglas in the film *Wall Street*. He bought and sold companies and dealt in shares on the American stock exchange. Martin Sheen played Bud Fox, a stockbroker who admired Gekko and wanted to work with him to get to the top. Gekko's rapid decision-making seemingly delivered fantastic results every time. There are many other films in which quick-fire decision-making is applauded and the hero gets just about everything. If we have been exposed to such stylised management approaches they certainly leave an impact on us and become part of our mental models.

I was speaking to someone recently about this concept and it was only when she was actually swimming with sharks in some exotic holiday destination that she realised that Sean Connery's ability as James Bond to swim faster than sharks in *Thunderball* was a complete fallacy. A little too late, I think. (More about mental models in Chapter 6.)

We are wired to think we get things right and if it goes wrong we need to find out the lessons learnt to help our thinking in the future. How mad is that? How great would it be if we actually could look from the present to the future, explore the scenarios properly and prevent failure. I know at this point you are judging me. Well this isn't such a crazy idea.

Twenty years ago in the 1980s I worked in the automotive industry. We were busy implementing lean manufacturing, reducing waste and doing business process re-engineering. I am astonished today that the buzzword in service industries, especially finance and health, is LEAN – along with BACK OFFICE and six sigma – and the employees and managers talk about it as if it is the latest thing. (Most people we challenge don't know what one sigma is let alone six, but it's the right thing to say, apparently.)

One of the most impactful things the automotive industry introduced was something called planned preventative maintenance. PPM. We all knew that components failed on manufacturing machinery. We knew that statistically we could predict when this failure might happen. We didn't generally know the consequences of that failure, because it often depended on the context that we were in at the time. The PPM approach to this was to prevent failure, *think harder* about what we knew, replace parts before their statistical life was up, maintain things before failure happened. The impact was phenomenal. There was rarely a machinery failure on the line and I cannot remember hearing of an inquiry as to why something had gone wrong. PPM is not a cheap option, but it was orders of magnitude cheaper than picking up the pieces (literally) of a failed piece of machinery and the down-time that entailed. By investing at current cost we saved future costs. Now I am no accountant but that sounds pretty good to me in an inflation-driven economy. So we can justify thinking harder on cost benefit alone.

Let's think about an inquiry of which you may have heard. The Space Shuttle Disaster, more formally called the Rogers Inquiry, set up by American President Ronald Reagan in 1986. The space shuttle discovery launched from Cape Canaveral in Florida on January 28th 1986 and 73 seconds into its flight it broke apart leading to the deaths of its seven crew members.

One of my heroes, the late bongo-playing American Physicist Richard Feynman, was part of the inquiry panel. He was a real nuisance to the panel, asking all the simple questions that they didn't want asking. He was so annoyed by the whole process that he threatened to remove his name from the final report. In the end they allowed his views to be appended to the final report. They made for fascinating reading. Why? Well, simply, his conclusion was that the main rocket had been built back to front, or in his words "top down". Design the rocket and fill in the bits behind as required. If you don't recall, the failure to the rocket was caused by a small part, a rubber "O" ring failing on the right Solid Rocket Booster, because it was not designed for the job. The failure of the seal caused hot pressurised gas to be released that caused structural damage that in turn led to aerodynamic forces destroying the craft. Spectacularly Feynman demonstrated this by dropping a similar "O" ring into a glass of iced water, showing hardening of the rubber that had led to gas escaping from the booster rocket leading to catastrophic failure.

Feynman says:

"The Space Shuttle Main Engine was handled in a different manner (to other parts of the project), top down, we might say. The engine was designed and put together all at once with relatively little detailed preliminary study of the material and components. Then when troubles are found in the bearings, turbine blades, coolant pipes, etc., it is more expensive and difficult to discover the causes and make changes."

He goes on:

*"The Space Shuttle Main Engine is a very remarkable machine. It has a greater ratio of thrust to weight than any previous engine. It is built at the edge of, or outside of, previous engineering experience. Therefore, as expected, many different kinds of flaws and difficulties have turned up. **Because, unfortunately, it was built in the top-down manner, they are difficult to find and fix.** The design aim of a lifetime of 55 missions-equivalent firings (27,000 seconds of operation, either in a mission of 500 seconds, or on a test stand) has not been obtained. The engine **now requires very frequent maintenance** and replacement of important parts, such as turbopumps, bearings, sheet metal housings, etc."*

So here we are, working on something that had never been done before, using our existing thinking strategies to deal with the new complexities. Feynman was advocating the "thinking harder" approach before its time.

This is a tragic example of how preparation up front and thinking harder with a bottom-up approach could have saved the cost of the inquiry but also more importantly lives. The biggest message we are pushing right now is that your existing thinking strategies are insufficient to deal with issues in transformation especially if that transformation is linked to the catastrophic financial events of 2008/09/10 – because we have never seen it before!

Assuming that we can use existing thinking strategies in transformation circumstances is a costly mistake.

The point is well made in a number of other cases. The Fraser Inquiry into the Hollyrood Building in Scotland had a starting budget of £1.2m. The UK Hutton Inquiry into the Iraq war cost £1.68m. Later, Sir John Chilcott launched another costly inquiry to "identify lessons that can be learnt from the Iraq conflict". When things go wrong we can always find the money and the time to sort it out. Does this not make the world back to front? What if we put those resources, both time and effort, into thinking about the issues properly in the first place?

Politicians are masters at this, making statements to satisfy a need without deeper thinking and then having to spend money to mop up the problem. Do you recall the poll tax of Margaret Thatcher's government in the 1980s? What about the salmonella egg scare set off by Edwina Curry? Or indeed the MMR vaccination debacle of the 1990s. What about classification and declassification of cannabis in 2010? The list goes on and on. It seems we are wired to make decisions on new issues using existing thinking strategies and then only develop lessons learnt when things go wrong. The world is back to front. We can think about the lessons learnt before we even start if we just *think harder.*

I have found that trying to get people to *think harder* up front is a challenge. I can tell you many stories of Blue Chip organisations willing to give us half a day to determine overall strategy for the company, develop an international sales strategy, re-jig a dysfunctional board, work on site integration, and sometimes all of those together − "because we are too busy to get our senior people together for more than that". Typically at least one of the team will not turn up because they are double booked and they *understand* what the other meeting is about. At least one has to leave early because the CEO needs an email or a paper. The rest of the team fiddle with their PDAs for the first half of the meeting and leave to take calls. Unbelievable. When I point out to them the ratio of thinking time to implementation time, or the likely impact of not thinking harder about things they tend to slowly agree that they have more time and more budget available. We call the former behaviour *budgeting for failure*. "How much would we have to spend if we got this wrong?" is a question I often like to ask. "How much would we have to spend in order to get this right?" is of course the next question. The afternoon, assuming they can give us a full day, tends to be worthwhile as they begin to see the benefits of focusing and thinking harder about the issues. Often the time ends with them saying "We really need more time to nail this one," or "Why did we not allocate more time to this?" Sometimes you can't win!

So let's assume I have established that organisations do not spend enough time on thinking harder before activities are undertaken. I now need to explain that thinking harder doesn't mean spending longer or indulging evangelists like me. It's about using the time available to examine the reaction to proposals, reframe the strategies, align your "players" and work out what embedding it would look like.

Organisations exists in an action/reaction dynamic. Take an action and react to the reaction by taking another action. For goodness sake break out of this cycle, spend time thinking harder and make the outcome more effective.

So give me an example, I hear you cry? We once worked with a large integration project in a Health Board. We adopted the "thinking harder" approach from day one and the integration progressed without a hitch. "Fluke," I hear you shout. Well we worked with a multinational company using the "thinking harder" approach on an outsourcing project where they were going to off-shore the IT function. Using this approach they realised that they were planning to fail. Yes they could off-shore but the impact on the company was going to be too huge. An alternative strategy emerged of "strategic sourcing" leading to retention of key staff, retention of differentiated support services and in fact a greater bottom-line benefit than they had anticipated. The thinking harder approach has had a whole history of "flukes". We are just lucky, I guess.

So back to the world being back to front. Let's look at some other examples. Why on earth in the UK do we call the provision of health care "the National Health Service"? It is of course "The National Sickness Service". Why do we have accident repair garages not safer driving academies? Why do we buy "warranties" on products that should last a lifetime? Why do we have speed cameras and not speed limiters. Why do our children get sex education at 7 but can't begin to learn French until they are 11. We can't get speed bumps on a road until there is a fatality.

My favourite of all time is that when I sat on the board of governors at my child's school there was an opportunity to run a Cycling Proficiency Course on a school day. The board recommended to reject the proposal as a risk assessment had been done and there was too high a risk of children bringing their bikes to school who had not gone through a cycling proficiency course. What a mad world.

I was recently doing some coaching in an organisation and the person I was coaching told me they had just been given a new starter to induct. They had walked them around the building, introduced them to as many of the 200 staff who were in that day, told them where their desk was, showed them the canteen and the toilets and given them a health and safety sheet. They had then left them to give them some space on their first day. Does that sound familiar? Well shame on you. I suggested the induction was not about introducing them to the workplace – that is called familiarisation – but should be about them introducing themselves to you, their boss. Explaining what they needed to do a great job, establishing how they liked to be praised, how they liked to be guided, what their expectations were and what the support was they needed in order to be a good employee. Am I right in thinking no-one can remember the names of 200 people they have just met? What a waste of time. The induction was back to front and no-one realised it.

Let's look at some other examples. Why do people leave your organisation? Generally they have found a better job, better pay and better prospects. Sometimes it's just the context they find themselves in. In the inevitable exit interview you ask them about why they are leaving. It is surely the wrong question. The question should be of yourself. "What does someone else see in this person that we don't see?" That is a "thinking harder" question. The world is back to front; we do exit questionnaires to find out why people are leaving, not to challenge ourselves on what others see that we are missing.

Often the people who know the answers to the questions are the very last to be asked their opinion, if at all. In order to make transformation really happen, it's essential to focus on changing thinking. It's easy to get anyone to raise their hand; getting them to *keep* it raised means teaching them to think in a different way compared with the traditional way of just shouting at them to keep their hand up.

In many organisations, the people working at the coalface are rarely consulted about important decisions, when in fact their understanding of the situation, their knowledge of how things are done on the ground and their expertise in their area are all crucial to achieving success. Look at the National Health Service; they are obsessed with getting the waiting lists down, and they'll consult this expert and that expert, when the people they really need to talk to are clerical officers and nurses and all the individuals involved in the nitty-gritty of getting patients through the system as effectively as possible. They will tell you some of the real issues of getting patients' waiting times down. "Get the surgeons, doctors and anaesthetists to turn up on time." "Reduce meetings and stick to allocated times." "Contact patients before their appointment to ask if they are going to show up." "Continuity in staff handling patients." "Decide if we are counsellors or doctors." "Work to time." "Make hard decisions."

Across the board, the more senior managers are, the more likely it is that they make their decisions based on attenuated information – information that has been filtered through the various layers of management and condensed to one or two key performance indicators. Information that probably tells them nothing. Junior staff tend to make decisions based on a much wider array of available data in a narrower field. They are likely to make better decisions based on better data in their particular area of influence. Hand-in-hand with this comes a wealth of knowledge as to why things are going so wrong or so right. Organisations tend not to ask these people what they think as experience tells them that they will get a barrage of mostly negative points about the organisation. Hey, we don't want negativity now, do we?

We love negative people. We love positive people. But we really love negative people. Why? Because they are full of passion. They are motivated, opinionated, passionate and have a view. I recall working in a government establishment, I can't tell you which because I have signed the official secrets act, really! In this establishment we were discussing strategy. Before the meeting, the meeting owner took me to one side and said, "Jacqui is going to be in this meeting. She disrupts everything, dominates the thinking and should have 'we tried this years ago and it failed' tattooed on her forehead. We tried to get her *banned* from the meeting, but failed. Are you going to be OK?"

My response was "Of course. By the end of the meeting Jacqui and I will be getting on famously and she will feel like she has a real role to play."

Sure enough the meeting started off as usual with distrust, animosity and side comments from Jacqui. I let this go on for a while, not giving her much attention and then waited for the "we tried this before and it failed" line. Sure enough it came. I responded by turning to her and asking her simply to "Tell me more". Astounded she began to expand on her first statement. "This project looks like one we tried before and it failed." *"Tell me some more..."*

"The management team asked for our opinions and then ignored everything we said." *"Tell me some more..."*

"The discussion papers never got circulated and the lead on the project left at the critical implementation point." *"Tell me some more..."*

"The strategy was implemented before we were informed or engaged on the journey." *"Tell me some more..."*

"We were told to just do it and everything would be fine."

Wow, Jacqui was telling me a lot of interesting stuff about the way the company operated. The next question I asked was crucial. "Jacqui, imagine we got to a successful conclusion on this project. What would we have to do?"

"Establish a solid team, ask people their opinions, explain that the decision might mean our opinions are not included but acknowledge the fact you listened. Keep us informed by telling us the journey we are on. Tell us why things are changed, don't just change them. Accept that we will get some of this wrong and we will need space to change our minds. Don't assume as a management team you have all the answers. Show some vulnerability and understand why we sometimes show up as not on board. Invest time in asking questions up front..." At that point we all paused for breath. Jaqui's colleagues were amazed she was actually defining what needed to be done in a positive way. The list ran to some fifty-six statements. What followed was a discussion around those statements with the others and a clear definition of "things to do to get it right this time". The world is back to front. Involve the nay-sayers, not just the yay-sayers, up front. They will help you get things done and boy do they have passion if you can press the right buttons.

People have detail that is attenuated as it moves up the management chain. Decisions based on the attenuated data do not always translate well. How do we amplify the decisions downwards? We assume we use subtlety and intelligence; more often than not we use volume and instruction.

So how can we start turning it the right way around again? This is simple but not easy. Effort and commitment are involved.

- Recognise that thinking harder is valuable and time spent thinking about new strategies and challenging existing mental models is a cost-effective way of preparing for transformation.
- Your existing thinking strategies are unlikely to be suitable for creating transformation in your organisation.
- Embrace the people who are negative about the activity; they generally have insight into how to do things properly.
- Make yourself available and be in the meeting. Your job may be on the line six months from now if you don't.

- Put the world the right way round.

These are of course my own observations of how the world is back to front. You may be able to come up with many more.

5

Understanding Context

When was the last time anyone said to you, "So what's on your mind today?" I am guessing not for a while or never. It is simply not something we ask.

However, people are driven by context! To demonstrate this, first of all we have to give you our definition of context; Context is at the interface of an individual's internal and external life.

"I thought this was a witty business book not meditation practice," I hear you say.

Hopefully that is exactly what this book is. However, watching the world interact whilst having an understanding of context, environment and mental models is a powerful skill and one well worth developing.

Essentially understanding context is the skill of being able to put yourself into someone else's shoes, but being able to do that without judgement. It is about taking a highly objective view and not being surprised or frustrated when those involved may not be able to do the same. Going back to the introduction of this book, this is knowledge. It is knowing that a tomato is a fruit. Being able to manage context, environment and mental models within an organisation (essentially emotional management) is wisdom. It is knowing that tomatoes don't go in fruit salads.

In order to get a handle on this, let's give an account of what we see as context, environment, mental models and how these interact in separate events.

Context is, to us, where everything which is going on in an individual internally – their thinking, emotions, past experiences, learning through observation, learning through direct experience, i.e. our mental models and emotions – meet the outside world, our environment and the events taking place within that environment. It is where the rubber hits the road.

In the outside world there are separate events taking place all the time. Count how many events take place in your day; you get up and have breakfast (event one) you put your contact lenses in (event two); your youngest daughter trips over the cat and starts to cry (event 3); your boss calls on US time to discuss the "regatta project" (event 4).

Before you get to 9 a.m. there are so many events happening that you probably forget about most of them before the day's end (this is called filtering and we discuss it in all its greatness, as well as the downside, in the next chapter). Events are ongoing. It is the stuff that happens to us within an environment.

The environment in which you are existing when the event takes place is important. The environment is not just the place in which you are physically present. It is the culture, etiquette, people and personalities, physical properties, light, sound, smell, all coming together to form an environment.

It is well known that the environment plays a huge role in our behaviour. Take high school students, for example. In their home environment they may lounge around doing little or nothing, being uncommunicative, eating only noodles in their locked bedrooms blasting out Black Sabbath noises and screaming at anyone who gets too near telling them to go away. In contrast, at school they are reported to be studious, bright, highly sociable and polite. What has changed? Does this kid have a twin? No, it's all down to the environment which cues us to act in a certain way.

Finally we have mental models. This is the internal mix of past experiences, learning, both observed and practical, our family, culture, beliefs, goals and values. It is all the stuff which you carry around that makes you you.

So how do these interact, and what relevance is there in all of this to the everyday humdrum of business?

Think about the following, slightly obvious, situation. Three people in a car driving home after a music concert. Two boys (we will call them Steve and Gavin) and a girl (Laura) are friends who have been at the concert together (event 1). On the way home the car breaks down (event 3). They discover that it is because the car has run out of petrol; Gavin had passed the last petrol station saying, "It will be fine, it runs on fumes" (event 2).

While the same events have happened to each of the three individuals, we wouldn't be at all surprised if the following behaviour ensued!

Steve is fairly annoyed with Gavin but is committed to a strict regime of a half-hour exercise every day. Steve believes that this will be enough to pass a fitness test at the end of the month (mental model 1). Steve decides to take this opportunity to run home the rest of the way, about an hour's worth of exercise. This makes him indifferent to the current situation as he has now reframed it as an opportunity to fill his exercise quota for the weekend.

Laura is furious with Gavin as she is booked to do a shift at the local pub (event 4) and will now not be able to finish her uni essay before the shift. As she is incredibly studious, believing that this will earn her a first class degree (mental model 2), she cannot forgive Gavin for his stupid mistake. Laura also quite likes Steve and is a little irked at him running off.

Gavin is secretly in love with Laura and believes there is a chance that it could all work out between them (mental model 3). He was only due at his mum's house tonight (event 5). He is positively delighted at the opportunity that he will now be left alone with Laura and the broken down car!!

The first three events are common to all individuals but due to future events and different mental models at play, the behaviour couldn't be more different. Context is the space we find ourselves in, where our mental models and events happening around us produce emotions, which, as we know, drive our behaviours.

Having the insight into the context of Steve, Gavin and Laura gave us the ability to really see what was going on and completely understand the behaviours. To one of our three stranded individuals however the behaviours of the other two may have seemed at best odd, at worst very, very frustrating!

This little story illustrates some crucial points around context:

- People are driven by context
- Everyone's context is not the same even if the events which are happening to them are the same.
- Context can change rapidly
- Context is driven by events and mental models.
- Context contributes to emotions.

In organisational (or personal) transformation, to assume that everyone's context is the same is wrong. Unfortunately it also happens to be a fairly widespread human trait to greater or lesser degrees. Understanding that everyone's context is not the same is an insight into emotional intelligence, but that subject is reserved for our next book!

We have worked with some fantastic and some not so fantastic groups. On the whole there is always a degree of tension in the group, some more than others. Where does this come from? It comes from individual context.

We once worked with a group involved with transforming the HR function of the business. One individual (we shall call him

Jack) was totally disengaged from the project. Other members of the team kept rolling their eyes, tutting or generally just getting on to him about his behaviour. Jack tended to respond in a standard way which was to say something like "It will never work, what's the point?"

As his colleagues became more and more frustrated with him and conversation became heated, Jack also became more animated and dug his heels in more. From this we knew one thing: Jack had passion. The issues were not because he was apathetic; he was passionate about something and he would defend this to the nth degree.

As his colleagues became more and more frustrated and started saying things like "We don't have time for this" and "We just have to get on with it", we asked Jack what he would do if he were in charge of a project like this.

After sidestepping the question a couple of times he answered us with: "A plan, we need a plan and I'm not moving until we have one." However his team couldn't buy into this; from their perspective there was no time to write a plan. They couldn't see that by slowing the project down by perhaps a day, creating a plan and engaging the whole group they would move faster than they thought they could. Not allowing Jack to have a plan meant they were going nowhere. Jack had set up the proverbial camp!

At lunch break I had an informal chat with Jack. I was interested to hear where the need for a plan came from.

Jack was a man in his late thirties, fairly confident and obviously very intelligent. During our conversation I discovered that as a young graduate Jack had been asked to do something. When the project had dramatically failed and cost his then company thousands of pounds, Jack had been made scapegoat and as a young graduate with no record of why he had done what he had done, he had been an easy target. From this it was easy to understand Jack's behaviour. It was all down to context, and

Jack's context surrounding projects and plans was complex.

Context however does not need to be relevant to the topic in which the individual is engaged in order to have an effect on the way they show up. When people are brought together to resolve an issue, come up with a solution to a problem, do some strategic thinking or to be told about a decision which they will be asked to implement, rarely does anyone understand their context, yet we judge them on their behaviour.

As individuals enter the room they carry with them a whole host of stuff, mental models, current and upcoming events, home life events and past experiences of a similar meeting. They do not walk in with a fresh mind.

We were intrigued by this insight and decided to put our theory to the test in some senior board development meetings we worked on throughout 2008 and early 2009. The dates are important as the recession had really just bitten and organisations, especially financials, were under huge pressure. The following are some of the statements we collected when we handed out some post cards on which attendees were asked "What's on your mind today?"

People filled these in anonymously and either handed or posted them back to us.

- I am worried about my sister's new puppy which is sick.
- I can't get over how badly my team played in last night's match.
- I hope this meeting goes OK (meeting organiser).
- How many times do we need to do this? I thought we all got it last time we met!
- I found out today that my IVF has failed for the second time.
- My husband lost his job yesterday. He is redundant. I don't know what to do.

- I'm going to be a dad!!!!!
- What time is lunch? I suffer from low blood sugar.

Imagine these people in the same room faced with a large-scale organisational transformation task! These were the thoughts dominating their minds at the moment in which we asked them. How do you think the behaviours would have played out? How do you think you would react to such behaviours without the inside knowledge of what was really dominating thinking during the meeting? I guess, like us all you would react a little differently if only you knew the true context.

Now, of course, you can't have one-to-one coaching and counselling before every meeting. Nor do we anticipate that your staff, peers and boss would want you to know such deeply personal thoughts. The point is this. Monitor your reaction to behaviours and ask if you know the real context in which that person finds themselves. You do not need to know their full context in order to empathise with them and reserve judgement on their behaviour.

Now on a less personal note and in the same meeting, let's add the following context into the mix:

- I know our budgets for this year are shot, I've just no extra resource to put into this project.
- I don't know what to do next. I feel really stuck.
- I am so excited about this project it is going to be great.
- I think this project is terrifying, it could so easily go wrong.
- If only they would commit the resource to this project, I feel I could get involved.
- I don't understand what all the fuss is about. We did something like this before and it was fine.
- If we don't get this one nailed I will be feeling a tap on my shoulder I think.

- We have no chance of doing this by December.
- Well as long as it is done by March things will be fine.
- I am going to nail this in a week as I've been here before, I think.
- I have a conference call to make in one hour. If this over-runs I'm in trouble.

So in this list of thoughts we can see not everyone is on the same page regarding the same project. The group's contexts surrounding the environment of the organisation in the event of the project are very different. Normally there is never the opportunity in such meetings to discuss "context"; the tendency is to get straight into how do we do it?

Unless you know where everyone is, what their understanding is of what they have been asked to do and how they feel about doing it, how can you progress? How can you work with behaviours which, from your perspective, may seem irrational?

Giving people the opportunity to talk freely about how they feel, the scope of what they are trying to do, the behaviours they recognise in themselves and others can really open up the group's context so that it becomes an open book which everyone can see. If everyone can see the collective context of the group then behaviours are more easily understood and can be met with helpful responses rather than unhelpful reactions.

Secondly, ask people how they feel about the task you are setting before you ask them to think harder. Having the opportunity to tell you how the world looks from their perspective and not just about the task in hand, and feeling like they have been listened to goes a long way towards changing thinking priorities to favour what you are asking that person to do. We have seen too many meetings to count where people just jump straight into what the meeting is about without giving everyone in the room a chance to get their heads straight.

We were once working within the NHS in a straightforward thinking-harder type of session. One of the key people called to say she would be late. As it happened she arrived only twenty minutes or so into the full day session. Typically she would have been expected to just join in but we could see that she was flustered and her head was certainly no way near being in the room.

We stopped the meeting for an unscheduled coffee and checked in with the lady. It turned out that her 10-month-old baby was sick and she had to reorganise childcare before attending the meeting. It was hugely abnormal for her to be late for anything so the whole experience was stressful for her. During the coffee beak she was able to let her colleagues know about her context and she visibly started to relax. We started the meeting again, explaining React, Reframe, Align and Embed (Chapter 1, for those of you who need to remind yourself) to our client group, using the story of a poorly child to illustrate our points. The latecomer was able to laugh as she saw the absolute relevance of what we were saying.

In this case, the opportunity to share context was enough to completely take the stress away and allow this person to perform at their best. Having respect for her context meant she was far more likely to engage in our session.

The other thing we see is organisations having little or no respect for people's time. Meetings over-run and people are just expected to stay regardless of their context surrounding catching flights, buses, trains or being home in time for children. Organisations rarely if ever pick up on a behaviour and allow the person to attend to the event which is causing their context to be stressful.

We are going to look at a fairly frivolous example but will then take it up to a higher level of importance.

Suppose that I know my road tax is due, perhaps even days

late, and I am in a meeting. You ask what's on my mind and, because it's the kind of environment where it's OK to say "my road tax" you will, in an instant, have insight into my context. You are also a great manager and suggest that as no-one else is here yet, I take five minutes to do it online before the meeting starts or you write it in your diary and promise that you will remind me at the end of the meeting and that it's OK to sort it out on company time!

Where do you think my thinking priorities would be during this meeting? Still on my road tax or engaged fully in the conversation?

Let's take it to a less trivial level. This time my context is that my partner has just been made redundant. There was an announcement last week that HR (where I work) was to undergo an efficiency review and myself and several team mates have been called to a meeting with my manager. I have been with the company for only a couple of months.

The manager's agenda is that he does need to make HR more efficient and he has selected some of the newer team members, me included, who have been with the company for less than a year to tell him about how things worked efficiently in their last place of work to see if he could learn anything from them. He also knows that once people have worked somewhere for a long time the culture becomes the norm – perhaps the newcomers could shed some light on where they have seen the inefficiencies in this organisation. The order from above is that this task will not involve any redundancies.

Two people's contexts: the manager asking for insights and the new employee being asked for observations. What emotions and behaviours would you see? What is my context given what is dominating my thinking, my partner's redundancy? How engaged am I likely to be in the meeting? Can you spot what might happen next? I am sure you can and this is all down to context.

So the manager, being not such a great manager, starts the meeting by telling us that we are all new in the organisation and that we don't necessarily know about the culture here. He asks us to tell him about the inefficiencies!

At this moment I feel a huge internal reaction, with the thought of making it external!

You may think that this is unbelievable, but this actually happened in an organisation we worked with. Thankfully we uncovered that one of the people being asked for their opinion was consequently off looking for a new job when actually they were considered to be part of the "talent pool".

One of the places where we see the importance of context played out more than anywhere else is in one-to-one coaching. Often we deal with senior people who have been labelled "difficult", "aggressive", "obstructive", "poor communicators" or simply "underperforming".

Inevitably, these coaching sessions are not about "adding" something, improving skills or coaching in the traditional sense of the word. More often than not we take something away, we dilute the angst within the individual and allow them to see their own behaviour which subsequently brings about a change in thinking.

You see, the context of many of these seemingly "awful" people is, sometimes, quite unbelievable. Often they are dealing with issues both at home and in the workplace that would cause many people to be signed off with stress for months. The problem is that these individuals have a different strategy in dealing with their context and the demands being made of them; they come out fighting, shouting and bullying anybody they come across. Their mental models dominate their reaction to their context.

The fascinating thing about this area is that, once you start talking about context with them and the individual rapidly feels listened to, things start to transform.

Of course we do not recommend that anyone without substantial expertise puts themselves into such challenging coaching positions. However, the lesson to be learnt from these individuals is that they are not intrinsically bad. They have context which, combined with the requests being made of them (the environment), leads to undesirable behaviours. Fortunately, for most of these individuals, they were been rated as technical or functional genii by their peers and therefore time and money was invested in them.

Unfortunately that is not always the case, and often the "difficult" people in organisation are never really given the space in which to change their mind. We hope that highlighting the issue of context to you in this book begins to change all that.

How do you find out about someone's context? The questions that you ask are very important. The biggest lesson here is to ask questions which are without context themselves, so that the respondent may fill it with theirs. This way you find out what is on their mind, not what is on your mind! There is a distinct difference.

How many times has someone from your organisation or an external organisation asked you what you think? It's not uncommon but what tends to happen is that there is an agenda someone wants to know about something. The something does not necessarily fit with what's important to you. The something is usually what the board "thinks" might be preying on the mind of its staff. Rarely does that something match with reality.

We once were brought into an oil and gas company to find out why staff were becoming less and less engaged with the vision of the organisation. A staff engagement survey which was sent out on a quarterly basis threw no light on the subject other than to say that staff were becoming less engaged.

The problem with the survey was that it asked questions

which interested the organisation. It did not provide a platform from which staff could be heard.

We met with some of the senior guys. It was clear that engagement was very important to them and they had some ideas on what the issues could be. They felt that a change which had been implemented eighteen months earlier had not gone down well with some of the staff. However they just couldn't seem to get the staff to tell them how to fix it. They had asked around 100 people for their opinions about the recent change and nothing untoward came back.

The senior guys had decided that the sample was too small and only by engaging a much wider slice of the organisation could some real insights be gained. We advised that we should talk to several smaller cross-sections, face to face, before a large-scale online session was conducted across the entire organisation.

The results were quite amazing!

Staff told us quickly and easily what the issues were. Firstly the main bone of contention was not surrounding the 18-month-old change but a major change implemented in the organisation over ten years before which had had such an impact on some of the staff that they were still "reacting" to what had been done to them. They just didn't feel as if anyone had ever listened to how they felt and how marginalised they now saw themselves to be.

The second great insight was that the engagement surveys were making things worse! The staff saw them as some useless management waste of time and money. They said they couldn't tell us what even one person from senior management looked like as they didn't even have a photo to refer to. They were angry at the fact that no-one, until now, had bothered to meet them face to face and ask them what was on their mind.

The senior members had been too focused on asking the questions they wanted to ask. The questions had been full of context (important in doing a snappy survey) and this left little room for the staff to add their own context.

Questions such as "What do you think is the best thing to come out of project zack?" and "On a scale of 1 to 10 please tell us how much you enjoyed the recent 360 reviews?" lead and direct thinking. They do not dig around in thoughts dominating thinking.

Have you ever seen questionnaire questions like this:

- *On a scale of 1 to 5 how excellent has our service been?*
- *Given the immense cruelty of fox hunting should it be banned?*
- *Pollution is a major cause of climate change. Taxation is one way of controlling emissions. On a scale of 1 to 10 would you support using taxation to improve our climate?*

I know, ludicrous, but we have all seen similar things.

If you really want to know someone's context, keep the question as context-free as you can. For example: "What's on your mind today?", "How do you feel?" and "Tell me more". These are mainstay questions. It is hard to get into the way of not adding context onto the end e.g. "How do you feel about the integration of site c and site b?"

Try practising at home and catching yourself as you try to add context to the end of questions. In a short space of time you will find that it comes more naturally. When first setting up Miascape and embedding the approach I wanted to take, I frequently asked cashiers at supermarkets "How are you today?" and from there "Tell me about that." You would be amazed at the amount of context material I could gather in the time it took to check out the weekly shop. I never approached any of the retailers with my findings but if anyone from the big four is reading, please get in touch, I think you will find your staff response interesting.

Understanding people's context is central to the "thinking

harder" way of doing things. This emphasis is represented even in our company name. Miascape is an anagram of I AM = MIA and "scape" is another word for perspective.

Organisations often instigate change without having worked at understanding the context of all the people working within the change. Without that understanding, it is impossible to move these individuals forward on the personal journeys of engagement, change and transformation that are necessary to effect real and meaningful transformation across the organisation as a whole.

Often, when people appear to be exhibiting resistance to change, or in response to orders coming from their leadership, what they are really saying is: "You don't understand my context. If you give some of your time to understand my context then you will understand why I behave the way I do in this environment."

Understanding context, rather than focusing on behaviours, is key to becoming able to change the way people think.

At the same time, as individuals we are not always consciously aware of the complexity of our own context. We operate on our front-of-mind information and we are consumed by that information, repeatedly working the same things over and over. By digging deeper, realities and motivations that lie beneath the surface of more obvious facts and contexts can emerge as extremely important.

To dig deeper and reveal the context we need to ask the big open question: "So that...?"

6

The Future Landscape

Seeing the future has been a desire of humans since the dawn of time. We can all appreciate how useful it would be to be able to see into the "land of what lies ahead" for us. A few individuals profess to have this gift but for the vast majority of us the future is unknown, un-chartered and just a little bit scary.

We do, however, possess a vastly underutilised piece of "wetware" that allows us to visualise the future, our brains. Our brains are, by design, capable of immense acts of imagination albeit some brains more than others. We have all imagined scenarios, events, actions and reactions. Just think now for a moment about holding the winning lottery ticket for a second and then think about your future in light of that. Bang, you were there, no crystal ball required. Of course this future may not happen but we do, on the whole, have the ability to look forward to the future. In our experience this ability to move our minds to the future is rarely put to great use. A quick glance towards the future may be made when project plans are being written but rarely are individuals, teams or entire organisations, asked to imagine themselves in the future and to explore what that means. Scenario planning is best described as "guessing a trillion futures" what I am proposing is thinking harder about being in that future that you want to happen not second guessing every possibility.

The other thing about the future is that when people, teams or entire organisations are asked to think through a step which they are about to take in support of reaching that future landscape, often the thought processes fall short. We use front-of-mind images rather than thinking harder. How do we know that? Well we have worked with enough people to know that without some sort of stimulus or process the thinking stops short. Often thinking concentrates around what might go wrong and all too often this is a very linear thought process which only takes into account perhaps one or two foreseeable issues around your desired future and then follows those events linearly. The exploration process is rarely, if ever, creative, free flowing, taking into account not just the negative issues which may arise but also what would happen if things went really well, the positive aspects. The thinking rarely expands to what might happen in entirety within your specific future.

In our experience, often most problems are caused by unexpected success where the outcomes are sometimes too positive. We plan for failure and rarely plan for success. For example:

We want to sell our new product X. We have come up with all the things we think could go wrong and have made contingency plans. We are ready for the plant going on fire, the delivery of raw materials being late and the production manager being sick. We then decide to launch product X. What happens? Things are great, we are selling more of product X than we ever imagined. However we didn't plan for this and are struggling in the "back office" to deal with the orders; we only set our supply chain up to deliver 120,000 per month but our orders are now double that. We have an idea for a sister product that we think could be even bigger but we have no time to work on this. Things are awful. Our customers have left us because we couldn't deliver their extra demand. The sister product has since been launched by another company and guess what, it's twice as lucrative as product X. Essentially the lesson to take from this is that we rarely think hard enough about the future landscape we want to get to. We do the easy thinking.

In our experience, humans are cognitive misers. We don't like thinking harder for very good evolutionary reasons and if we nail ten possible points of failure we think we have done a great job. In chapter 11 we learn how the cognitive miser learns to think harder again!

The next logical point to make in this chapter is that once we learn to picture our future landscape it will bring with it a whole bunch of emotional reactions. These reactions may be hugely positive ("I can't wait to get to that future") or immensely negative ("I just can't go there, I'll have to leave the organisation/ team/group"). The reason people react differently towards a change is down to the experiences that they carry around in their heads. We use experiences here in the widest sense in terms of direct experience, what you have heard, learnt, who has influenced you, what beliefs you carry. These past experiences largely govern the strategies that the individual will adopt in the future. We call these mental models.

These mental models are not based in logic, providing coherent prescriptions of behaviours and reactions to any given context. No, we are human and therefore not always logical. The other crucial element of these mental models is that they are stored by us knowingly or unknowingly and often with lots of emotion surrounding them. Let's just think for a minute about how we acquire these mental models and how they may come into play when we look towards the future. We, as humans, are like sponges and we take stuff on even when we are not paying attention to it. How many times do you find yourself singing a jingle from an advert only to discover that you have no idea what the advert was trying to sell?

We absorb experience, where we went to school, our friends, our family, our dislikes and our likes, our beliefs and values, the films we watch, the music we listen to, past experiences of organisational change or an experience relayed from a work colleague about a programme that we were not part of but nevertheless have the benefit of their experience. Included in all of these are emotions. Even if we are hearing about a friend whose marriage has recently failed, we absorb some of the "stuff" of the experience. We are also liable to take on, at least in part, how they feel about it, their emotions. Emotions are incredibly powerful, they are driven by our thinking, our mental models. In turn our emotions drive our behaviour. Without understanding the thinking and emotions behind a set of behaviours it is impossible to just get that person to stop behaving in that way. Their thinking and emotions may be so deeply rooted that the individual isn't even aware why they do what they do.

As a keen horse-rider, I recently attended a horsemanship clinic, run by Dr Deb Bennet, a palaeontologist and excellent horsewoman. During a classroom session Dr Bennet showed us a very old film of the first Lone Ranger episode. For those of you too young to remember even the repeats, this is where the Lone Ranger, an archetypal cowboy, and his side kick Tonto, a native American Indian, get together. The cowboy story progresses to a point where the Lone Ranger needs a horse to ride and in the space of 30 film seconds the two of them rescue a wild white stallion, patch him up, train him to a point where when the lone ranger shouts, "Silver, come." Guess what? The horse comes to the Lone Ranger as if by magic. Now even those of you who have never touched a horse before can see both the romanticism and also the fundamental flaw in all of this. It is just not going to happen that way. It is stylised, idealised and time compressed. These memories are still in my head after many years and I have to remind myself when I see a wild horse that this memory is not reality. A little piece of me still believes, as I did as a child, that a horse can be rescued and trained in 30 seconds. It is so hard to shake off. What "miracles" have you seen in your lifetime that have been embedded in your mental models as facts? Let's challenge "overnight success", "sweet boy turns bad girl good", "one man/woman saves the world", "amateur with no experience beats the consummate professional", "banks give money because they like you". A large part of our mental models is based on experiences that are just not true. But we like to think they are.

When this is pointed out to me, my logical grown-up head can override such memories and imprints, as I now know it takes months or years to do this miraculous Lone Ranger task. However, notice the word "override" and its implication that we need to be aware of these time compressions and falsehoods, and consciously correct their attempt to pervert our mental models. Of course, all the emotions of the 3-year-old child are still with me; that is why I still ride horses, but at least as an adult I recognise that!

For those of you with children or grandchildren or if you are a concerned uncle or aunt, please do not ban the kids from watching or listening to stories. Stories can be incredibly powerful and are an important part of life. All we intend to do here is to make people aware of thinking, mental models and experiences. Just by noting this you will be far better equipped to challenge your own emotions and thinking around change and transformation either in the workplace or at home. What stuff have you absorbed from experiences of your organisation? Even those that you know to be flawed or untrue. Do they still influence your thinking? Or has your thinking been over ridden by something else? Are the emotions still there? When someone talks of a future similar to this experience how do you feel? Are you aware of what is running your thinking about this potential future? The chances are that, until now, you hadn't given it much thought.

If an entire organisation is exposed to an event which creates within the individuals a shared set of beliefs (e.g. when X happens Y soon follows and Y makes us feel bad), when a similar experience arises the shared set of beliefs will form part of the thinking strategies and will therefore drive behaviours. The individuals may or may not be aware of their thinking; the belief sets would have been created from their perceptions of the event. We cannot say that the belief sets were wrong because they were drawn from the individuals' own perceptions, so how could they be wrong? However we can take time to uncover why people are behaving the way that they do. By discovering what thinking and beliefs drive the behaviour we can begin to empathise with their perspective.

So where does this lead us? If we can understand why someone thinks and behaves the way they do, we are in a far more powerful position in relation to understand how they may react to the future landscape. If we spend some time thinking about how people may react and interact with the future landscape, what will be going on at an emotional level, then we are far better placed to make adjustments or allowances, or simply give time and space in which to allow the individual to change their mind. The future landscape can be a scary, exciting, unknown but inevitable place. We always travel to the future, right? Spending time thinking more deeply about what that may look like can truly inform decisions taken on the way to that future landscape. Understanding what we are actually doing to people emotionally when we ask them to move towards a different future landscape from the one they were expecting is incredibly important. If we do not understand and manage thinking and emotions then we are unable to manage anything. It is interesting that traditional management and leadership styles shied away from any mention of emotions. Dealing with how people felt was seen as a weakness, a lack of control. However, the opposite is true. Unless you deal with the emotions of your staff you have no control whatsoever. The veneer on the surface may indicate that everyone is moving along with you but at any given moment the emotions will emerge and derail your agenda.

However, this mental journey of considering our future situation is not without its side-effects.

Firstly, the experience itself can be quite emotional, and depending on what that future looks like, people can exhibit positive or negative emotions in the here and now.

Picture a door, it is green and surrounded by a stone wall. There are plants climbing up the wall. I ask you to go through the door. Dependent upon your experiences (both those you have personally been a part of and those you have watched and learnt from) you will have a different take on what walking through the door means.

If the last time you went through a door like this one you discovered a beautiful garden, and the sight of a similar door brings back vivid positive memories, smells and sounds of that experience, now you will find yourself happy to walk through the door and even quite impatient to do so.

Suppose, however, that the last time you walked through a door similar to this one, you discovered two ferocious dogs. Once through the door it had slammed shut behind you and you were subjected to what seemed like an eternity of barking ad snarling dogs. It was a terrifying experience. Just seeing a door similar to that one brings back the painful memories. You even find your heart-rate increasing just at the mere suggestion of going through it. There is no way on earth you are going through that door unless someone can convince you that it is a dog-free environment!!

The second thing about the future is that describing your

future situation to someone else in conversation makes it easier to explore that future, i.e. what would it feel like, smell like or sound like?

Try using the word "landscape" to define the current situation you find yourself in. Describing one's current landscape can be done quite easily and unemotionally. If asked to describe your current landscape, you might say, "Well, I'm at the airport bookshop and I'm just leafing through this book to see if I want to buy it," or "I'm at home, relaxing, reading..." If, instead, you were asked, "How are you getting on with transforming the way you live and work?" providing an accurate answer could be quite a stressful business.

Let's go back for just a second and introduce the concept of "landscape". Landscape is simply what you see around you. It is external. It's not how you feel or react to what is around you; it is purely what's there. What can you see? What can you hear? What can you smell? For example, if you were to ask me about my current situation I would be likely to talk about trying to write this book in time for my publisher, my children are coming home for tea and I am so frustrated as my PC keeps crashing. I'm very annoyed at the roofer who hasn't turned up today and the cost is going to be huge and in this recession you would think, wouldn't you, that the roofer would need the work and PCs would work properly!

Yes, you would probably receive a rant about how I was feeling rather than an accurate description of my situation. It would include emotion.

If, instead, you asked me about my current landscape and gave me the example of "There is a cup of coffee on the desk", I may be more inclined to continue with: "There are two dogs lying on the rug. It is raining and there is a hole in the roof. It is nearly five o'clock. I am writing on my computer. There is an issue with the computer. I am writing a book. I am writing chapter 6."

The emotion is less intense and we can see the wood and the trees for what they are – that is, statements about my situation. Current landscape, a clear and accurate description of the world around me. Current landscape is crucial in transforming organisations, especially when, as discussed earlier, several people may be inclined to see a "situation" in a different way depending upon the emotions that are being shaken up by that situation. If we can, instead, get individuals to talk about current landscape, very quickly it is easy to gain some sort of consensus of what the landscape looks like. The views may not match perfectly but at least you won't find some people shouting "mountains" and another bunch of people shouting "beach".

Knowing where you are at any time is a big step in achieving a seamless, sustainable transformation. The next step comes from gaining a real insight into where you want to go. By focusing on landscape, we can imagine how we want our future landscape to be. We can ask questions like, "If you achieve the change that you are looking for, what will your landscape be like?" The answer might be something along the lines of: "The organisation will be running smoothly and making a profit. We'll have streamlined our services and everyone will be working together well." Then, we can ask, "And how did you achieve all this?" Having envisioned this future landscape, we can perform the exercise of looking back from this perspective and asking ourselves, "What did I need to do to get here?"

In order to bring about transformation either in a business or personal space, first we need some real understanding of how things are going to look once we have transformed. How will we know when we have succeeded? What will we be able to see? How will it feel? What will be the big signs that will tell us that we have arrived at our desired destination? Imagined situations can cause all sorts of problems. Back to me at my desk on a wet afternoon – let's see what happens if you ask me about my situation and what could happen;

"I am sitting here and the roofer has turned up, finally. He seems to be about twelve and I'm not sure he even listened to me. My kids will be home any second and there is a chance they will start playing around the ladder belonging to the roofer. I am going to get really stressed especially when the roofer can't fix the problem. Oh, I don't know, maybe he will fix it and it won't be too bad, but I'll never get to karate on time with the kids!"

So as my imagination gets going I can create a whole host of things that might happen extrapolated from the situation I am currently in. If however I am confined to talking about fact, landscape, what is actually in front of me, my imagination finds it difficult to get involved.

"The roofer has turned up; he looks young. The children are home." So, using the word landscape can be incredibly helpful in establishing the factual "where are we" without getting too much emotion involved. It can have a truly calming effect even at an individual level. Try describing your current landscape to yourself the next time you find yourself in a frustrating situation. Do not allow yourself to talk about emotions but only about facts of what is happening in front of you.

Imagining the future from one's current landscape is difficult; creating a mental image of that future landscape and then acquiring a retrospective gaze provides us with a more meaningful perspective on all the steps that must be taken to achieve that future.

How wonderful it would be if we could all have the benefit of hindsight today!

People are obsessed with looking into the future, what is going to happen between now and then. People often have some idea of what "then" may look like. However their thinking is unlikely to have gone any deeper than "one day I would like to buy a holiday home in France". Often, because little or no thought is put behind "how we get there", the dream never becomes reality or it takes much longer than it might have done with some hard thinking!

In organisational transformation people often do not want to engage in the future because, as explained earlier in this book, the perceived change to their world is traumatic or the challenges faced appear too large to navigate.

We often use the analogy of trying to climb a mountain. Standing at the bottom unable to see the summit due to low cloud, the task looks ominous and even impossible. There may be one or several reasons why you would think that you couldn't achieve the objective. To you, standing at the bottom of the mountain, it all seems impossible, foolish, a waste of time if not dangerous to attempt this feat.

If, however, your colleague has taken the route successfully and is now standing at the summit looking back down towards the bottom, able to see you in all of your angst, they would probably be able to inform you that actually it looks harder than it is. These are the big things you need to overcome and this is how I did it.

We can all take this mind journey into the future and imagine what that the future landscape may look like. By doing this we see the barriers from the other side, i.e. "this is how to get round that issue" instead of "we can't do this task because of this..."

It is truly amazing how thinking in this way frees up the mind. Try it with any simple issue where your first reaction is "I'll never be able to do that". Instead, take some time to think harder! Put yourself forward into that position of success and then coach yourself as to how you got there. What did you have to do to make it all possible? What were the big steps? What did you have to look out for?

Return to your present time with this information and plan your way forward, out of this impossible task with the benefit of hindsight!

The same is often true of organisations. Often there is a "vision" but more often this is a statement about where they want to be. There is usually no depth, little acknowledgement of how this may feel, sound, taste, and certainly there is almost never any real understanding of how this new world may feel, sound, look to other individuals, groups or the organisation as a whole.

Most people would like someone else to tell them what that future may look like. Actually engaging someone in thinking about that future for themselves is much harder because the process requires a much greater amount of thought and effort from the individual. This process feels hard, frustrating and challenging, almost like discovering a new type of puzzle and no-one has told you about the rules or strategies you should employ.

If you ask someone what they would do if they won the lottery, they will usually have an idea. If you then ask them to tell you what that looks like, feels like and sounds like, they will need to think a bit harder. If you then ask them to take themselves to that place, to actually give themselves the pleasure for a moment of thinking about how it will feel, look, sound, be in their new world and then to consider what advice they would give to other would-be millionaire lottery winners on what they should do to get to that place – the advice is likely to be free flowing and more informed than if you had simply asked them how they would become a lottery winner in the first place. Tactics for choosing numbers, checking tickets and a policy on spending would all be part of this embellished advice.

By taking our thinking forward into the future, challenging ourselves to think deeply about what that future may look like and by then looking back towards ourselves in the dim and distant past as if to give advice on what are the first, second and third steps are to being successful in such a quest, then we are thinking harder. We will be far more informed about what we are doing to do. We will have measures which will show us that we are moving in the right direction and perhaps most importantly we will have knowledge of what the first step is, and how and when it should be taken.

Most manufacturing organisations will already be applying this kind of thinking in their supply chain management. However, in the implementation of change they rarely take this approach and often find themselves in one of two places. Either they are trying to implement a change and they find themselves dragging their people along with them or, and perhaps more potentially damaging, they are about to implement a change – they have announced this to their staff; their staff are on board and ready to start but some final decisions have not been made so they can't tell their staff about the finer detail. Weeks and months go by with little happening but corridor gossip. Susan returns from a year's maternity leave and notices absolutely nothing has changed! The apathy among staff is now so bad that the change is abandoned as the world has moved on and the change is no longer relevant.

How likely do you think it would be for this group of people to get on board with a future programme of changes? Yet it all started out so positively; what went wrong?

The senior team should never have announced the change until they had thought through both a positive outcome and a negative outcome to their announcement. They had expected a negative response from their staff and had not made final decisions in light of this. When the response was a positive "Let's go", they were caught out and found themselves behind their staff saying "hang on" instead of leading their strategy from the front. Looking towards the future landscape and communicating what it looks like for you, asking what it may look like for others, clarifies and explores the unknown. The unknown is your enemy, creating lots of emotion as old thinking strategies come into play. Make sure your future landscape is thoroughly explored before you set off on your journey.

7

Baking the Cake

In this chapter we are going to explore the fundamental difference between change and transformation. Is there a difference? Well there is if we say so. That is not arrogance it is more about clearly defining what it is we are talking about so that others understand the language we are using. How often do we fail to do that when we start a new venture?

Twenty years ago as a raw business re-engineerer, I distinctly remember listening to Michael Hammer, the "inventor" of re-engineering, on BBC Radio 4. I worked in a large corporation in the business systems department as a business systems consultant. I thought I had made it. I had the word consultant in my title. This implied of course that I could be consulted – about what, I was never so sure. We were just implementing standardised business systems in the manufacturing environment and were looking at how to get things done rapidly.

The standard approach of the senior management team was to sit in a room, decide what to do and tell people it was going to happen. (It's becoming a repeating theme in this book isn't it?) My role was to try and implement *change* through implementing business systems. Basically technology-led *change*. Get people to do things differently by computerising it.

I remember working in one of the group companies where a radical MD was in place who had cut his teeth in British Steel. His number two was an equally dominant personality. As an aside, I remember them communicating between their offices, which were actually next to each other, by fax. This was before extensive email use, but really! The point of all this is that they had thirty-two identifiable *change* initiatives in place in the organisation in order to transform radically the performance of the business. Each of the *change* initiatives had an acronym and none of them delivered what was expected of it at all. They expected the staff to engage with all of the initiatives and deliver the benefits that had been determined in the board room. This was in the same organisation where, when a new canteen was built, ninety percent of the condiment sets disappeared and there was a regular replenishing of the cutlery in the canteen. Engaged staff? I don't think so.

As I recall, this was also the company where the security guard refused to come out of the hut at the entrance to the factory and visitors had to leave their car and go to him. Even if they were at the factory to negotiate a £1m contract – another example of back-to-front reality (see chapter 4). The senior management team referred to themselves as "The Power House". That said it all to me. No-one else called them that, just themselves. Now that is worrying.

Change plans happened on a regular basis. Edicts were issued on a regular basis; ideas flowed and things were commanded from the Managing Director's office through The Power House to the staff. But nothing really changed. There were so many initiatives that the staff became immune to them, and the strength of the words in the communications became stronger and stronger as the hyperbole lost its intensity. "We need to change" went to "We must change" went to "It is imperative that we change" went to "You're fired if you don't change" ...No, they didn't get to publicising the last one, but it was often said in meetings.

During that period of the 80s and 90s my experience of working was that people wanted to *change* things. They approached it by deciding what to do and then just telling people to do it. They expected them to comply, and if they didn't they would tell them they had an option. To do it or not. So they'll do it, right? Well, for a while they will. People will comply until you stop measuring or monitoring, and then they will revert back to where they were, or fairly close to it. That is change. Unfortunately my recent experience of large organisations is that they have learnt very little in the last twenty years. Whilst they talk about people engagement they are still struggling to achieve it.

So why does this book challenge conventional thinking?

If you google "change models organisation" you get 21,900 responses (November 2009). If you google "transformation models organisation" you get 3,550 responses. So there is something about language here that we need to address.

Whenever we give talks on change and transformation we always get challenged by someone in the audience as to whether we have come across the "Wazinksy Popplethwaite model on organisational change" that they swear by. Or the systems based thinking model by "Wobblebottom and Crutch" which is "awesome". These are made up, obviously, but you get the picture. Someone always challenges our approach by throwing some favoured change model in our face and expecting us to defend our position. We never do. Why is that? Well, let's talk about change models for a while.

Change models tend to be based in the dimension of time. The classic change curve – do I need to draw it? – is so linearly based it is painful. It is still taught in business schools as being the *de facto* standard of change. It treats change as a transition from one thing to another. A repeatable act. A one-dimensional activity with clearly definable points along the journey of how everyone will *feel*. And the starting point is always anxiety. It also has no relevance to the enthusiastic in the team. It is simplistic and easy to apply, but has no depth or life of its own. "It's just like marriage really – seems great, honeymoon period over, can I see a future, let's get on with it and make a go of it." That is exactly how I was taught it at business school. Sadly in my case the marriage analogy didn't quite work, but that's another story.

The traditional change curve is easy to understand and can be applied in isolation. That's why it is so widely used. But it is insufficient. It is like describing the universe in terms of a mechanical device. On one level it works, but it fails to capture the complexity of what is really going on.

Let's look at the other simplistic models of change. Many of them talk about unfreezing the organisation, changing things and then refreezing the organisation. Now if the organisation is one man and a donkey taking people for rides this is easy to do. Close the donkey rides for a day. Change the donkey for a horse. Re-open for business as a horse riding school. All you have changed is the mode of transport. There has been no real transformation. No really, try unfreezing HSBC or BAT, IBM or Microsoft, Walmart or our Public Organisations... changing something and re-freezing it again. It is impossible. The organisation is so vast and dynamic that trying to get everyone to stop, change and then go again is surely impossible.

What about the rapid redesign change models? Focus on what you can do, do it and then get on with it. Wow, that's rapid. Again, it's the "doing to you" stuff. "We can move people to Bristol." "Let's organise it." "Let's do it." That's change. Do it to them, do it fast and it will work. No it won't!

As Shrodinger and Heisenberg those great scientists have said, "the world is not an orderly cosmos, it is semi-chaos that we can only understand in part." A simple model of change is inappropriate to describe what is a hugely complex structure. We need a complex model that helps us understand what is happening when we talk of transformation. But by complex we do not mean complicated. Just rich.

Organisations that follow the classic change curve take the "well, they'll get used to it or leave" approach. There has got to be something better.

Let's try and define change a little more deeply. Change is independent of the direction of time travel. What does that mean? If you take a video of two pool balls colliding and moving apart, it doesn't matter whether you run it forwards or backwards you cannot tell which is the right way. Change is like that. You could easily move from where you are back to where you were and people would think you were making progress.

When change happens spontaneously it does so because the new arrangement is more probable (the most likely natural outcome). It is "probable" that a ball will roll downhill. When it does so, nothing has fundamentally changed. The ball has just moved to another position on a slope. Imagine an infinitely long piece of guttering on which there is a slight slope. Place a ball mentally in the guttering, a red one, and let it begin to roll down the guttering. Remember this is infinitely long. There is no background, just the guttering suspended in space. The ball rolls along the infinite guttering. Now take a mental snapshot and store it. Take another, take another. All the pictures look the same. Why because nothing has really changed, The ball has just moved to a new position in the same environment. This is called a quasi-stationary state. No matter where you snapshot the changing position of the ball the picture looks the same. That's change.

Remember the 32 change initiatives in my old company? They were in quasi-stationary state. Anyone looking in would see change initiatives and activity which looked just like the change initiatives and activity if they had looked in a year before.

Change can be instant but not permanent. It can be reversed and reversed again. It can exist in a quasi-stationary state so that nothing seems to change. Change models describe single events and simplify what is a hugely complex environment. In short, change models short-change organisations wishing to learn about transformation.

Think of this. We have a number of ingredients on a table to bake a cake. Our children are in the kitchen with us. The phone rings. We leave the kitchen to answer the phone and in our absence the children move the ingredients around on the table top. We come back in and see what has happened. We are methodical people and like things to be in the place we want them; without hesitation, we put the ingredients back to where they were on the table, ready to bake the cake. Change is when something is altered but can be randomly or purposefully put back to where it was. No change model says that. So what about transformation?

When we look at change models they are always designed to describe taking something, modifying it in some way, and then stabilising it in the future. The word "different" springs to mind. Reducing waiting lists in the NHS is target-driven and is generally achieved through a change. An example being not putting you on the waiting list until your appointment has been confirmed. This could easily be changed back. In order to hit targets for GPs that you are seen on the day you call in for an appointment, in the UK, you cannot make an appointment for the following day. This was recently reported in the Daily Mail a UK national newspaper

"PATIENTS are being banned from booking advance appointments with GPs so surgeries can meet a Government 48-hour waiting time target, it emerged yesterday. Practices are meeting the official pledge by only allowing people to make an appointment on the day they call the surgery. This ensures that plenty of appointments are always free and GPs' diaries are not

cluttered up weeks ahead."

This is changing the service to match targets. Both the targets and the changes can be easily reversed as they are functional and affect behaviours not the thinking of individuals or the organisation.

So what is transformation? Transformation is when something happens that cannot be reversed. Further if we were to film the transformation, we would intrinsically know which direction was forward, something that cannot be said about change. So where does baking the cake come in? Well, imagine us in the kitchen again with the ingredients on the table. We leave the room and the kids mix the stuff together, stick it in the oven and we come back twenty-five minutes later to find a beautifully baked cake on the table. The ingredients have transformed. They are in a form that cannot be separated back to the constituent parts either purposefully or randomly. The cake has been baked and a transformation has taken place.

How can we extend this analogy to transforming organisations. Well, clearly whatever we do in behaviours can be reversed. If we ask someone to stamp a document on Monday or Tuesday they can stop doing it on Wednesday. The documents will just look like they did before. If we ask people to change their behaviours and answer the phone saying "Acme Services Ltd" instead of the old "Acme Ltd", they may do so, but by the end of the week they may have reverted back to the old ways. If we tell nurses to call patients "clients", pretty soon they are calling them "patients" again.

Clearly transformation within organisations is not going to happen through change because all change does is change actions and behaviours and procedures. Something that can always be reversed.

So this is where organisations sit. They come up with actions and try to get people to transform. But they just change. This is because they do not engage their staff and change the mental models, the beliefs and assumptions that their existing staff bring to work with them. Nor do they transform the mental models of the new staff they recruit. They generally focus on the "we do it differently here" approach – just "do" what you are shown how to "do" and you will be fine. Since when has the induction process for staff focused on the mental models of the new staff member and how they may be at odds with the way the company likes to operate? Never. Organisations have focused too much on the behaviours of their staff and not on the mental models they carry with them.

So let's go back. Think of the red ball rolling down the infinite guttering. Remember it's infinite. Take a snapshot, now take another. Suddenly the snapshot is of a duck sitting on a duckpond quacking away. That's transformation. It's not a blue ball or a steeper slope. It's like a dream, teleporting to a new place. Show someone the duck and tell them there used to be a red ball on guttering here and they will laugh at you. It's absurd that you could think such a thing!

Transformation is about changing the mental models that people carry so that their belief sets change so that their behaviours change so that their interaction with the environment changes.

Once an individual transforms their thinking and gets insights they rarely, if ever, revert back to the old ways of behaviour. They just can't. What is more is that no-one told them to change. They made this decision that something had to give in their own thinking and that is why it is so powerful.

Let's look at some examples. The desire of people to lose weight is a classic problem. Sure we can change their behaviours. We can get them to weigh themselves every day, calorie count, eat healthy food, exercise once a week, join a slimming club, have their stomach stapled, but this is all doing things to them to change their behaviours. The real success is if their thinking is transformed by gaining the insight that they will live healthier lives if they exercise, they will live healthier lives if they eat well and they will be alert and full of energy to tackle the world if they combine the two. If this healthier lifestyle is seen to be enjoyable, almost addictive, then thinking will transform and something very different will happen. The behaviours will no longer require bashing from a diet or slimming club in order for this person to keep going. Their motivation will come from their own thinking. Real success comes from a thinking change not from a behavioural change.

Let's look at smoking. Smoking is easy to stop. Just don't light the cigarette. However, millions of people carry on smoking. Why is that? Because their thinking models allow them to do it. Only by transforming their own thinking can they give up forever.

How does this relate to organisational transformation? Well, the answer to this one is simple. The organisation behaves like a collective of the individuals. The organisation contains a number of individual mental models; it therefore needs to transform these mental models, not just change its behaviours. If leaders continually try to transform organisations by targeting behaviours they will fail. They must transform the thinking. Baking the cake is the same as transforming thinking. Moving the ingredients is just change.

8

Engaging Language

This book is written in English. If we are very lucky and it gets translated into other languages then I am guessing that this chapter is the one that will have to be revised the most. Why is that? Well, this chapter is about the language we use to communicate. It is about how language changes, how definitions change, how organisations ascribe meanings to words and how we have personal definitions of words. It is about how words can be the stumbling blocks of progress and they can be the catalysts of transformation. Words. One of the ways in which we communicate thoughts, ideas and intentions to each other. But how do they land and what words *should* we be using as we try and move through transformation?

Words have powers far beyond their immediate meaning. They are laden with symbolism. The words that we choose to use in explaining even the most everyday things convey volumes about our view and presuppositions about everything from social class to cultural background to hierarchies at work to perhaps a less than conscious reluctance we feel towards doing something that we know has to be done. When someone says "Are you really going to do that?" what they mean is "I wouldn't do that". When you say "I am going to jump out of an aircraft in a wing suit", one of my ambitions by the way, the response I get is often "Why would you do that?" What is really being said is "Why would *I* do that?"

People cannot NOT communicate what they are thinking. Reading what is behind the responses is a skill you can develop. Just try it. Listen to what people are saying and ask "Why are they saying that?" "What must they believe in order for them to respond in that way?" This is a really insightful skill to develop. Firstly it stops you immediately reacting to what is being said, but secondly it gives huge insight into why they are behaving in the way they are. It tells you about their *thinking.*

In the UK there is much snobbishness about the words "tea" and "dinner". My friends from the South tell me that dinner is something that you have in the evening and my friends from the North tell me that dinner is something that you have at mid-day. In the North supper is something that you eat just before you go to bed and in the South it is a meal that is less formal than dinner. Even though it is now politically incorrect, in 1982 I once asked my friend from Hayling Island (that's almost in France it is so far south in England) what the ladies were called who worked in primary schools to serve the lunches to the children. His instant response "Dinner Ladies". Point proven, northerners are right.

If I told you whilst writing this book I am "reight po fagged" unless you were from Lancashire (I am) you may not know what I was saying. Simply put, "I'm very tired." In less dialectical language, I would be also within my rights to say "I discovered my table as I removed the table cloth." I obviously knew the table was there so it was no surprise, but dis-covered literally means "to take the cover off". When did its meaning change to something more abstract? I have no idea. As mentioned in an earlier chapter, the word "nice" once upon a time meant exactly the opposite. To be "thrilled" literally meant to be pierced through. Words change.

William Shakespeare is credited with inventing many words including *puking, lacklustre, bloodstained, unhair,* to name a few – the last did not catch on and has disappeared from use, but I am intent on bringing it back! We would all struggle if we consistently invented words in isolation, although we have introduced a unique vocabulary in our company.

"Sickciting" – the feeling of anxious anticipation.

"Electronical" – probably has a circuit board in it.

"Confusement" – the state of being confused.

"Newme" – it's not brand new but I've never owned it before.

These are words which we use all the time in our own company. This book may mean that they can be absorbed into the general vocabulary of the nation.

Guy Deytscher in his book *The Unfolding of Language* refers in some detail to how metaphor has modified language. Trouble is *brewing*, anger is *simmering*, resentment is *boiling*, people are *seething*. Metaphor is an important part of our language. Descriptive terms are powerful and add colour to our sentences. Another interesting point he makes is that metaphors generally flow from concrete to abstract and not the other way round. We say a meeting is "tough" but no-one yet says a steak is "severe". Our language evolves over time and in the thirty years that I have been involved with business I have never seen a dictionary of "what we really mean in this organisation when we use certain words" printed. People in the organisation absorb the meaning given to words by their exposure to them or they apply their own definition to the word and merrily move along.

I remember an occasion at school when I was given a calculation to do. The instructions started off with "given a piece of wood of unit length..." I had no idea what this meant. I knew that wood could be measured in inches, something newfangled called centimetres, it could be a yard, a meter, a rod, a pole, a perch or a span. But a piece of wood of *unit* length. What did that mean? I approached my maths teacher, a Mister Bancroft, and said "Sir, how long is something of unit length?" He looked at me astounded. "Bury," he said, "if you don't know the answer to that, I have been wasting my time with you." I didn't know the answer and submitted my homework incomplete. When I was summoned to "See Me" it was explained to me that something of "Unit" length meant one of any measure. It didn't really matter whether it was in inches, miles or light years. Unit length meant one of anything. I felt foolish and the fact that I am relating this story now means that it had a huge impact on me.

Words have to be defined before they can be used for meaningful communication. When did anyone ever say to you "So Deirdre by *change* we mean... by *transformation* we mean... by *success* we mean... by *failure* we mean... by *support* we mean... by *development* we mean..."? I can hear you shouting at the book now. "We actually define these in documents we write." But the whole organisation does not see the documents. It is generally a small group who understand the words that are used and the definitions ascribed to them.

The French. I love them. Their language is controlled centrally by the Government, or at least they try to control it centrally but words creep in and the language changes. One of the things you notice about French speakers is that they will quite happily correct your grammar should you stray from what is correct. However they have less words than the English language and hence words in French can have many meanings. One I found particularly useful when renovating a house was baguette. We Brits tend to think of a baguette as bread but actually it just means stick and can be applied to anything that is stick like. However the French have an interesting response to hyperbole. When language is overused it tends to lose its effect if it is initially a powerful metaphor. The French consider "très" (very) to be sufficient to talk about an intensity of emotion and balk at things like Hyper, Super, Mega, etc. However, they use them extensively in their colloquial language. Hyper Marché, Supermarché, Mega Marché.

We are guilty of diluting impact too. We become immune to "strategic imperative", "transformation of this organisation", "customer excellence", "exploiting the market", "delighting the customer", etc. At one time these phrases would hit us with the momentum of an express train but now they are sloganised and we barely notice the intent behind the words. We become desensitised to words the more they are used and the more we are exposed to them.

So not only do organisations use words that have not been properly defined; they assume that their definition is the same as others' definitions. Words over time migrate their meaning and lose their power. Organisations wear words out and end up struggling to gain impact resorting to stronger and stronger metaphors. An apocryphal story goes that Fuji, the film company, had a mission statement that evolved into "Kill Kodak". Wow that is strong.

People hang onto language too. They assign values and objects to language. They assign beliefs and assumptions to language and they use language as a barrier to moving forward. They get wedded to labels and titles, they get wedded to descriptors and most of all they get wedded to the things they like. Changing language causes reaction as much as making requests of people causes reaction. I remember the furore as Jif cleaning products moved to Cif cleaning products. Marathon chocolate bars changed to Snickers and Oil of Olay changed to Oil of Ulay. There was uproar. Why? The product hadn't changed. The efficacy hadn't changed. The price didn't change. It was just the word associated with it. People do not like the world to which they are aligned to change. When the message about all these name changes started to filter down it became apparent that it was a rationalisation of product name across the global brand, so our understanding began to change. Now, of course, the new names are completely accepted and many people don't even know what a Marathon bar was. However, I occasionally still wander into the shop and ask for a Marathon and a look of consternation crosses over the face of the teller. "A what?" they say.

In one organisation in which we worked we were pulled up for calling the females in the group "girls". We were told that the word "girls" trivialised their role in the room and projected an image of them that was frivolous and unprofessional. Whoa! That's a new definition of girls. We were further corrected that "you would never refer to a group of men as boys would you?" Well actually I would. "Come on, boys, let's get this task done" seems a reasonable expression to me and one I would be happy to use. Time for some coaching. We explained that the definition they had given to the word "girls" was theirs, not ours. They had not shared it. They were correcting us for the implication of the word that they had defined rather than asking us what our definition of our use of "girls" was. We asked them what other language they used to which they had given a unique organisational meaning. This exercise took some time, I can tell you, as they produced a whole list of words that had unique meaning within the organisation that they failed to convey to people working within or outside the organisation. Interestingly enough "workshop" was one such word. A workshop was a place where the team went to give their views and the facilitator pulled the material together in a coherent piece. That is not our definition of workshop, but we began to understand why this organisation resisted our attempts to get them to do the harder thinking and align on the topic of the day

We also worked in an organisation that was in conflict. The respective teams, from the new organisation and the old organisation were struggling to develop as a team. The reason? Well after two days of meetings it finally occurred to us. It was the language that was being used by the team members. The language was causing conflict. The newcomers objected to people referring to the "old" names and the old organisation objected to the labels that were being used by the new team. The solution? It was easy. We defined a set of labels and definitions that were acceptable to both teams and they started speaking to each other and the transformation progressed. So it wasn't what was being asked, it was the language being used to describe it.

When this dual language is not tackled it creates issues and is divisive. Often there is a difference of origin – for example, Saxon and French. This has class implications as well – in times gone by, Saxon words were used by the proletariat and French words used by the posh folk. When organisations transform, rarely does their language transform, but it is a good place to start transformation as it creates new joint definitions, reduces conflict and raises understanding. You can even use the existing words but agree on the definitions with the whole team. Remember "dress down, chinos, black dresses and all that." Dress down in our company means jodhpurs or motorcycle leathers. Imagine the reaction if we walked in to a multinational dressed like that on their "dress down" day.

However don't jump in and change language just yet. Another example of the power of words comes up in organisations every day. People feel listened to and respected when the issues that concern them are initially discussed using their own vocabularies and expressions, rather than reinterpreting what they say and filtering it through another's language, subtly changing meaning and emphasis along the way. It is also hugely important to understand the power of words and expressions used within their specific cultural, temporal and personal environment. Why do people choose to use the words they do? And what do they really mean?

Our experience working in organisations going through transformation is that people generally do not feel listened to. Why is that? Well one of the biggest reasons is that when individuals tell their story to anyone they never seem to hear the same words coming back. For example, we have heard on numerous occasions members of staff saying something like "I am totally hacked off with this change initiative" and the facilitator or meeting owner playing back "So you are frustrated by how slow the project is moving." Excuse me, but that isn't what he/she said!

When organisations take a "thinking harder" approach they begin transformation by listening to the organisation and playing back to the organisation what it hears in the organisations own words. This is a failing of most organisations and it is certainly a failing of engagement surveys. If I say the management team are a "useless load of freeloading graduates", I need to hear you say that back to me to know that you have heard. If I say "The management have transformed the culture in the organisation", I need to hear that back. If I say "all meetings are a load of bollocks", I need to hear you say that back. I do not want to hear back "Our staff say that 30% of meetings fail to reach the outcomes defined." I want to hear my comments and thoughts in my language. That's what I understand. My language. It's like me saying to you "I would like a cold beer please" and you replying to me "Sie wünschen ein kaltes Bier ". I just wouldn't recognise what you were saying. When we capture material in meetings we always record literally what has been said. At first this is hard. When we first began using this approach I remember the first time we had to write "we are crap at meetings" on a white board. Something felt out of place. But the person that said it laughed out loud and said "That's the first time anyone has listened to what I say!". One more engaged, one more fluke.

In transformation, listen to you organisation and play back what you heard to them in their language. Do it either in the form of "you said 'I would like a cold beer please'", or play it back in the first person. Repeat "I would like a cold beer please". It is so powerful.

After you have listened and played back in the language of the individual or the organisation, new words can be introduced to talk about the future, and only then can you start collectively defining and understanding what this means to the organisation and the individual. It is at this point that we advocate defining what "future" means, what "current" means, what "success" means, what "performance" means, what "client" means, and so on. It is the time to collectively define the language of the organisation.

We always begin our interaction with the organisations we work with by listening to them and working out what the language of the organisation is. This gives us the opportunity to ask the stupid questions about the acronyms that inevitably get thrown around. We work in so many sectors that the same acronyms can mean different things in different organisations. SMT equates to Senior Management Team in one organisation and Sales Management Team in another. Even though we are external suppliers we get severely (should that be toughly) corrected if we don't know the language of the organisation.

It is only when we have listened to the organisation in their language and played it back to them that we start to introduce our language to help them define the process of transformation.

I am going to share some of our language with you here.

Current Landscape – This is a description of the place that you currently find yourself in. It is a factual description of the landscape you see around you not the actions that people are taking.

Future Landscape – This is where you want to be. It is a description of the landscape that you would like to be describing to others in a fixed period of time, say five years. It is not the actions that people are taking.

Imperatives – Those things that need to be done in order to achieve your future landscape.

Mental Models – Those frameworks you carry around in your head that help you interpret the world. Everyone's mental model is unique. That's because the journey we have all come on to this point has been different. The mental models frame how you interact with the world. They are unique but hugely powerful in allowing you to cope with the multitude of interactions.

Climate – The things you can do nothing about. We find people in organisations spend an inordinate amount of time raging about the things they can literally do nothing about. It is a waste of energy. The story I always tell is that I love to motorbike. If I wake up in the morning and it is raining, I can do nothing about the rain. But I can still decide to motorbike. I should be focused on the riding and getting back safely, not trying to work out how I can prevent it raining. I can't, of course. It's a climate thing. Similarly we can do very little about the fact that we will all die at some point. A climate statement. In organisations, recognising climate statements with groups is hugely powerful.

Substantive – Things that are truly significant. "My car only has two wheels on it" is a substantive statement if you wish to travel somewhere in it. This contrasts with...

Emotive – Things that are based on emotion (literally, things that inspire emotion) and are often not substantive. If I tell you "I prefer to travel in blue cars" knowing that your car is red, this is an emotive statement.

We have a language of transformation that we use and define. What is your language of transformation. Does anyone understand it? When did you last define it? If you used the words Mega, Super, Substantial, Hyper you are on a loser before you start.

9

Making Transformation More Probable

Things happen. Sometimes we are surprised that they have happened and sometimes we expected them to happen. Our birthday comes around every year. We tend to expect this as it is on the same day every year. It is pretty predictable. Our car breaks down occasionally. We actually expect that our car will break down at some point but we don't really know when. Our ability to say when it will happen is less than saying when our birthday will happen. It is less predictable. Being hit by a road cone that has been catapulted into the air after a dog ran out of a house that had been left unlocked and ran into the path of an oncoming 52 bus that swerved and hit the road cone is not very predictable at all. Of course, the longer the sequence of events then the less predictable these things become. But what is predictability? How do we inform ourselves about whether something is going to happen in the future? Well, we observe, we collect data, we calculate. We analyse the *probability* that something is going to happen.

Every event has a probability associated with it. Here is an example, a simple example: Toss a coin and predict which way it lands. Heads or Tails? Were you right? Well, the probability of it being a head is 0.5 and the probability of it being a tail is 0.5. (Probabilities of all the alternative outcomes of an event always add up to one.) Toss the coin a hundred times and it will be roughly 50 heads and 50 tails. Now that's interesting, isn't it? I use the word roughly because I have tried this a number of times and NEVER got 50 heads and 50 tails in a hundred tosses. Why is that? Probabilities of events are just that, probabilities. It should happen like this but it may not. Now over time and a thousand million tosses divide the number of heads by the number of tails and you might get 0.9999999999999999. So it is pretty accurate and holds out our theory but it only gravitates to the theoretical probability after measuring *loads* of events.

Every event has a probability that it will happen. It may be a large probability, it may be a small one, but it is a probability nonetheless. A phrase I often hear is "I'd better do it today, I might get hit by a bus tomorrow." I actually went away and calculated the odds for being hit by a bus in Edinburgh, my home town. It actually worked out at 2 in a million. So the chances of being knocked down by a bus are greater than my chances of winning the lottery, 1 in 49 million but much less than having identical twins which is about 1 in 250. That assumes of course that there is a high probability that someone actually wants to make babies with me.

Now this is all theoretical. So let's throw something else in there. Ask 200 friends (you do have 200 friends don't you?) to pick a number between 1 and 10. Now statistically (a much over-used word) you would expect 20 people to choose 1, 20 people to choose 2 etc, but they don't. In fact it has been shown that they are not likely to choose 1 or 10 but likely to choose 3 or 7. Why is that? Well the answer is that people aren't perfect, as we well know. They have prejudices and mental models. They are certainly not random. Any choice they make is made on "reasons". Ask someone to pick a totally random number. I just did writing this book and they said "4". I asked them why? The answer was "I was going to choose 6 again but I thought no, I'll change it to 4." People are not random; they are driven by internal and external written and unwritten rules. Random events have NO rules behind them. I would argue that computers cannot generate true random numbers as there is always an algorithm behind it. They look random but aren't.

So just for interest here are some probabilities I have collated. They may be right, they might be wrong, but it was an interesting exercise:

- 1 in 12,000 to score a hole in one on an 18-hole golf course for an average golfer.
- 1 in 1.64 people in America eat breakfast.
- 1 in 10,790,000 people who fly will be involved in an airplane crash. (I have always been frightened of crashing not flying!)
- 1 in 8,730 that I will die of septicaemia this year. (Blimey.)
- 1 in 1.03 households have a refrigerator.
- 1 in 4 chance that an adult has been on the internet an hour before going to bed. In my house the latter is 1 in 1 chance. It's a certainty!

Ok so let's move on. We have established that events have probabilities that they will happen. Now let's look at outcomes of events. What is an outcome of an event. Well if I get married what is the probability of my getting divorced? (Clearly if I don't get married I am not going to get divorced.) If I make a million widgets in a factory, how many of them will carry a fault and either not get to a client or be returned? For the purposes of this book, consider the following key question: "If I enter into an organisational transformation what is the probability that it will be successful?"

Interestingly we try and calculate the outcome of an event by sampling previous events. So for the divorce example we would say, "Let's look at 100 marriages and see how many end in divorce." For the manufacturing example we would take a sample of 100 widgets and see how many were defective. If 1 in 100 of those widgets were faulty we would say that the chance of a widget being faulty in production was 1 in 100. Simple isn't it?

The accuracy of our predicted odds changes with the sample size we take – obviously.

Also, things that we measure have a natural distribution of values. Take the height of people or the length of time we shall live, or the length of our stride. The results fall in a range that a long dead chap called De Moivre called the "normal distribution". If we look at height data for males in the UK in 2007 the average male height was 1.772m. But there are people taller and shorter than these values. There are just more people round about those sizes than 1m tall or 3m tall. But it is possible for people of this size to be found. They are just rarer.

Some events are so rare that the chance they will happen is very small, but they COULD happen. Tossing a hundred Heads in a row, for example – very unlikely indeed, but theoretically possible.

What we have been dealing with up to now is the unhampered world, the natural world, the world without interference, the world without massaging or influence. We can make things more probable by influencing the parameters of the event.

What do I mean? Let's take horse racing. There is evidence to suggest that a powerful sedative, acetylpromazine (ACP) has been administered to horses prior to racing in order for them to go slow or even be pulled up in the race. This would obviously benefit gamblers in the know if the horse was considered a favourite. I also apply ACP to my bearded collie before clipping as it makes it more probable that he will stand still and allow us to cut his hair.

We can make it more probable that it will rain by seeding

clouds. Silver iodide and dry ice are sprinkled into clouds to generate ice nuclei or condensates that cause the humidity in the cloud to precipitate. Another example from my childhood experiments that has always fascinated me is the way you can get a sugar cube to burn by sprinkling cigarette ash on it first. This makes it more probable that the sugar will ignite. Don't worry, we are not going to get into thermodynamics or catalysts or hydrocarbons here. The message here is that we made it more probable that events occurred as we wanted them to.

A quick note right now about the word "manipulation". When the horse-dopers dope horses they do so to manipulate the outcome and gain from that manipulation and win. They do this by someone else losing. We call this a win/lose outcome. Win/lose is always the outcome from "manipulation". When we talk about making event outcomes more probable we are talking about a win/win outcome. The individuals involved in the transformation on the whole win and the organisations wishing to transform on the whole win. Our approach of "thinking harder" is designed to ensure that the outcome is win/win and not win/lose. Hence making things more probable in our sense is ensuring a win outcome for all parties.

Transformation has two dimensions. One is the transformation we wish to effect and the other is the speed at which that transformation takes place. Change can be a rapid event. Throwing paint at a wall is not the same as transforming the feel of the room. Transformation, we are told, is traditionally a painstaking exercise. That is why most organisations opt for change and not transformation. But what if you could increase the speed at which transformation occurs to be equivalent to the speed of change? You would get the benefit of speed *and* the benefit of transformation.

So let's talk a little about the speed of transformation. Organisations have an optimal speed for transformation but they never know it. They define a timescale for delivery of the project but do not take into account the natural speed at which the organisation can go through transformation. They force the organisation through to the conclusion and are surprised that the activity is not embedded.

Let's think about this. Imagine an audience leaving a theatre. They have just seen *As You Like It* by Shakespeare at the Courtyard Theatre in Stratford Upon Avon. They have enjoyed the production and are chatting merrily as they emerge from the auditorium. As they move out, several things can happen. First, they can all rush to the doors and a crush ensues resulting in the whole audience apart from the ten or so people at the front virtually grinding to a halt. Progress is slow. An hour later the last person gets out. The second thing that can happen is that the whole crowd is talking so much that they hardly move. The doors are not fully used and the people leaving are those who decide they will just slip away from the mêlée. The whole audience leaves in four hours. The third thing that can happen is that they leave at the optimum speed. No-one stumbles, no-one stops, the flow through the lobby of the theatre is matched to the flow through the doors and the whole audience leaves in 30 minutes.

Using this analogy a little bit more, a curve emerges. As people speed up from slow to faster there is initially a decrease in time to exit; then as they get even faster the time to exit begins to increase as the crush begins. The inflection is the optimum speed of exit. It is natural to the building, the people and a million other factors. What have they just seen? Is it raining outside or sunny? Is the last train about to leave? Are the restaurants about to close? What is the average age of the audience and their mobility? Unfortunately we do not know these values for every (if any) audience and therefore the optimum exit time is rarely achieved. However, there will be an *average* exit time, but this is highly unlikely to be the optimum. Interestingly I should think that theatres are designed for average exit times not optimum exit times. OK, so don't stretch these analogies too far, but I hope I have given you some insight.

In organisations there is an optimum speed for transformation. What's yours? I am guessing you don't have a clue. Suppose a project is scheduled to finish in December. Let's assume we are at January, but the optimum transformation time is fourteen months. You are only ever going to deliver *change* if you insist on the December deadline. Unless of course you decide to do something about it.

If we just revert to people for a moment. It has been shown that in order to regulate flow in a corridor all you need to do is put some indicator in the middle of the corridor that the corridor has two sides. Crowds will self-regulate which side to walk on in relation to the direction they are walking. The side for a direction may change but it will self-regulate quickly. There is a fine example of this at Edinburgh Waverly Station where small waist-high metal posts at 10m intervals punctuate a long walkway from the main concourse to platform 20. The commuters naturally self-regulate. Another interesting self-regulation example: in order for people to pass through a door in corridor or walkway more quickly the answer is not to put a bigger door in but to put more doors in. The commuters will then self-regulate passing through the doors in one direction or another.

So how do we make transformation more probable in organisations? We do this by recognising that when people move through transformation they follow a set sequence of events that we alluded to in chapter 1, and we use this information to accelerate the natural speed of transformation to enable projects to be delivered on time or in fact before the deadline. Let's reprise that knowledge.

When anything happens to anyone, the phase they enter first is *reaction*. The nature of the reaction depends on the context they find themselves in and in particular the emotional relationship they have with the content of the event. The reaction of my mother, a season ticket holder at Blackburn Rovers, to Chelsea beating them 5-0 at the weekend was significantly different to mine, who have absolutely no interest in football at all, not even a little bit. The next phase they enter is *reframing*. They have to think through what is happening, apply existing or new thinking strategies and explore what the outcome of this event/challenge should be. The third phase they enter is one of *alignment* – ensuring that others around them are aligned with their own position on the event, attitudinally, culturally and strategically. The fourth phase they enter is *embedding*. This is when things become the norm again and we begin to tell stories about our emotional reaction to the event that took place.

How can we use this to accelerate transformation? First of all we have to acknowledge that this is going to happen to our people in our organisation. Organisations cannot put a cap on emotion and they cannot prevent reaction. Have you ever been outside a meeting where bad news has just been given? Whilst the meeting might be silent, the volume increases outside the room as people leave and discuss their reaction to it. This reflects the culture of the organisation and how they expect their people to handle change. Commonly, organisations then expect people to just get on with it and they are pretty much left to their own devices, or given a budget to pull some consultants in because that will fix it, won't it?

People solve problems with their existing strategy set and are rewarded not for thinking harder but for coming up with a solution from their existing thinking that "solves" the issue.

What about in a "thinking harder" world? Let's think about reaction first. Reaction is good. Whether the reaction is deemed positive or negative, the reaction is good. Why is this? Because it shows that individuals are emotionally involved in the topic or activity. One of the things we can do to accelerate transformation is cause reaction.

Being in a reaction phase is strange. We are vulnerable, capable of being influenced but often at our most creative. When we are in reaction we feel we are thinking clearly but often we enter a confused state where our thinking is not straight and our thoughts are dominated by previous solutions and experiences and the emotions which these caused.

Often organisations send out cultural messages that they don't wish to see anyone reacting in a less than positive way. Some organisations I have come across are so concerned about the reaction of their staff to an impending announcement or initiative, that they do nothing. They dither for months, and in one case years, until such time as the whole context has changed and the initiative is old hat and no longer required. The staff in this particular organisation however had been expecting something to happen, and when absolutely nothing happened it fuelled deep mistrust of management and ensured general apathy towards future change projects. Paralysis by fear of reaction is real and causes the greatest of all downfalls in business; watch out for it. and if you need any convincing of the point look back over the financial disasters in this country of 2008-2009; it's enough to make your toenails curl!

Our advice is for goodness sake give your staff, team, group, division something to react about, and then explore that reaction. Reaction is to be celebrated, it means you are off the starting blocks; you are moving up the probability ladder.

By exploring the reaction you will make it more probable that people come with you on the journey. Both the negative and positive reaction can inform and energise. Remember, the reaction is from the context in which the individuals find themselves, not what is being proposed. Mining the reaction out through simple questioning and discussion means that people can move on in the transformation. Too often the reaction is talked of in terms of resistance. This is not the case. It is reaction; learn to love it.

Secondly, in order to transform rapidly, new thinking strategies have to be developed and the filters of the old world removed. This enables deeper thinking, new strategies and improved actions and outcomes.

By demonstrating the limited effect of existing thinking strategies in the development of transformational solutions, harder thinking occurs and strategies emerge that were not previously thought of. Do not try and move people into reframing before the reaction is out of the way. If you find yourself saying something like "OK, let's all get on board with this and brainstorm until we get the answer," then the chances are that you and your staff are not ready to think along reframing lines just yet.

Reframing happens when all the reaction is exhausted, there is no more. If you gain the knack of mining out reaction in people, you will probably find that individuals start to lean into reframing naturally, wanting to talk about the future, thinking of opportunities or new ways to do stuff. Make sure everyone is at this point before you try to move from reaction. Even if only one person is still reacting, it is enough to wreck havoc in a team or department. If you start to believe that an individual is never going to make a transformation because of insights you have gained through discussing their reaction, then you and the person may need to seriously consider their continued involvement in the transformation. However, make sure you give everyone your best shot. Do not simply suppress reaction.

If you try and put a lid on the reaction it will just pop up elsewhere. Spend the time to ensure the reaction is exhausted before you move on. Remember "The world is back to front"? Reaction is the place you need to spend time if you want to make your transformation more probable.

After reframing you need to get aligned. If you don't you find yourself working on umpteen different transformation projects rather than just one, as groups splinter off to do their own thing in a wholly unaligned fashion. This process of alignment involves sharing language, definitions, expectations and intentions in the project, and understanding a common measure that you will all recognise "when you get there" (a simple date on a calendar is not enough).

After aligning then you can start to embed by identifying the key people who will be involved in delivering the transformation. Not the mechanics of the transformation but those people who can make or break the transformation. Those individuals you need on board to deliver the project. And guess what, as soon as you tell these people they will react and you will be off on the same journey with them. As we said, it's not linear, neat or simple. Transformation is complex with many beginnings and many ends.

Transformations are more probable if you recognise these four phases and deal effectively with them. React, Reframe, Align Embed.

Now let's come back to making it all more probable. In order to make transformation more probable you must allow and even assist people to react, you then need to work hard in order to reframe with the best possible thinking that you can push (and we mean push, find out how in the next chapter) your grey cells into. Then it's time to get more probability into the picture by ensuring everyone is singing from the same karaoke screen and finally make sure that you use all of that emotional energy to fuel the more tedious practical actions that will be the wheels of your transformation. This makes transformation more probable. I would say that if you do all this, your odds of a successful transformation are pretty sweet.

10

The Cognitive Miser Learns How to Think Harder

We say: "If you think like you've always thought, you'll do like you've always done and you'll get what you've always got." Changing the way we think is the key to behavioural change and transformation. We humans are cognitive misers, tending to filter out a lot of the information we encounter.

You may have heard the saying "Can't see the woods for the trees" meaning it's difficult to see the whole picture when you are so close to something. In our experience people often feel like this in business. It happened to us recently when we were trying to decide the best way in which to package our stuff and educate people in it. We decided that one four day course would be sufficient but then decided on two four day courses. After about an hour we felt like we had gone round in circles and were still coming up with the same old stuff.

We all tend to think to a level and then explore that level of thinking. This is a logical, useful and efficient way to think, most of the time. However it doesn't really free us up to think to deeper levels (as demonstrated in the above anecdote) or to think in a more random and creative way.

In this chapter we are going to look closer at these human

traits which serve us well in one instance but can appear as a design fault in another. Being a cognitive miser can be both extremely beneficial and also a bit of a drawback. How do we become such a miser? Do we choose to think less about stuff? Not exactly, it happens through attenuation or filtering.

Filtering stuff is incredibly important. We only have so much bandwidth in our senses and evolution has ensured that we pay attention to those things which may be of most use to us. We have all experienced the cocktail party phenomenon where we are listening to conversation but in our other ear we hear our name mentioned in a different conversation. This results in our attention being grabbed for a few moments while we decide if the second conversation is perhaps more important to us. During this time we will have completely missed what was being said in the conversation we were originally tuned into.

This demonstrates our ability to actively attenuate information. Sometimes it can work against us.

For example, when watching TV we can be so absorbed that we do not hear someone talking to us. We fail to switch our attention even if the content of what is being said is quite important to us.

Television has many powerful ways in which it engages its audience, some more than others. As an aside, when starting a new relationship, I realised that my new partner was not into television at all. I was not so into it but had been used to sitting down each night in front of a soap or something because that is how my old relationship worked. (I'm not saying one is right and one is wrong they are just different) The interesting bit for me was after several weeks of really not switching on I arrived home one evening, my mum had been babysitting. In the corner the television was on and turned up to what seemed to me an unbearable level. I tried to chat to my mum but found my thought processes so interrupted by the television that I had to stop, turn the volume down and start my conversation again.

My behaviour may have seemed odd to my mum who seemed quite happy with the TV'S volume. The kids groaned as I turned it down and complained about not being able to hear it. So what was happening here? Was I the only one in the room without a defect in my hearing? My guess is that my own personal filters could not cope with the Television noise whereas, as my mum is an avid soap fan, she found filtering out the television while we had a conversation perfectly easy. My mum was far more use to the background noise, it was commonly part of her landscape and possible it would seem more strange to her not to have the television on.

Going back to being absorbed in watching telly. Think about watching something which you are really engaged in, the final of X factor, an exciting episode of East Enders or an FA cup final match. The chances are you would struggle to pay attention to someone wanting to talk to you at this moment. If however you heard a really loud smash which sounded like cars crashing, the chances are your attention would turn. You would then filter out the television while you dealt with the more important issue. You would not be half listening to the television while you were looking out of the window to see if it was your brand new, carefully parked car that someone had smashed into.

The same can be said of the other senses. If you don't take sugar in your tea normally, try adding sugar to your tea every day. The first few times you do this the chances are you will not want to drink it, it will be too sweet for you. If you really want to test the theory, keep doing this for several weeks. If you have the will power to carry on in the name of science it will result in you filtering the sweetness to the point where it tastes normal to you. After this, as a healthy eating fanatic, I obviously advise that you wean yourself off the sugar again!

My partner currently has a detached retina and has been told that due to the area of the problem, surgery is not possible. However it is expected that his brain will compensate and fill in the gaps, ignoring the signals that there is something wrong in the centre of the image. The brain will filter the signals which are unhelpful.

At a far more serious level, this piece of human thought engineering can be life and sanity protecting. Terry Wait, kept in solitary confinement in the Lebanon 1987-1991, reported listening to music in his head during captivity. This is what became important to him during that time, this is where he directed his attention. The chances are that, mentally, he started to filter out elements of his situation. If he hadn't done this, the chances are he would not have emerged a sane man!

Imagine the reversal of this process. The world must have seemed incredibly noisy, busy and a bit crazy following his release.

How amazing! It's stuff like this which attracted me to the subject of psychology as an undergraduate. I still get sidetracked by reading about an unusual psychological experiment which reminds me what an incredibly powerful yet complex thing the human brain and the concept of thought is.

Like most things in life, there can be downsides to this amazing piece of human design. We can become so accustomed to things that our brain no longer pays any attention to the stimulus. At a simple level this can be an interesting concept. I had a friend whose uncle had lived abroad for many years. He spent most of that time eating the hottest curries he could find. Upon returning to the UK he found that he just couldn't taste milder foods. Medium hot curries were now tasteless to him. His taste buds had been desensitised to the hotness of all those curries.

At a more serious level, we can start to filter out stuff which we should really be paying attention to. Stories epitomised by

The Boy Who Cried "Wolf" are an examples of us unconsciously or consciously choosing to ignore changes to things that have become normal.

Currently we are in a recession. During this time I have noticed filtering taking place towards what both politicians and the media are saying. Words such as "economic crisis" , "crashing share prices" and "highest unemployment figures" twelve months ago made my insides turn to water.

Today the language is so common to me, the situation has been going on so long, that essentially I ignore such language. "Crisis" is now part of my life. If a politician wants to get my attention now he or she needs to come up with language that is different, language that will make me "sit up and listen" But is this such a good thing?

On a personal level it probably is. If I had spent the last 12-18mths feeling the same way as I did when I first heard about the banking crisis then I would likely be carrying a stomach ulcer by now. By it becoming normal to me it creates less and less emotion in me.

On the other hand, for the sake of my business, I really need to be concentrating on changes in language which tell me that the situation is turning for better or worse. The politicians, especially those in opposition, really want me to pay attention to what is being said. I would coach them to stop over using language such as "crisis" and "downturn" I am somewhat impervious to that now. The politicians need to communicate differently if they really want me to start thinking differently.

As an aside, one of the best pieces of advice I received about the recession and other such catastrophes was from Alistair Campbell, ex spin doctor for Labour. At a dinner one evening in Edinburgh, when the whole recession thing was really just getting started, he gave me two pieces of information which I hold very dear. Firstly, he said, crises are rarely really crises at all. Often both politicians and the media over react and use the word "crisis" when they really mean "something not too good had happened". Secondly, and for me most insightfully was that "Crises end". Now this, although just language, I find very comforting indeed. I have found this advice incredibly powerful during these hard times and I hope Mr Campbell doesn't mind me sharing this with you now.

So back to cognitive misers. Our brains collate inputs and then concentrate on the things that seem more important. We get rid of "white noise" in our life. This leaves more bandwidth for other things. We take things as "given" and don't really notice their existence unless they stop or disappear. However, we are also capable of filtering behaviours too. Behaviours, cultures and environments over time, can become normal to us or those in the same situation as ourselves.

In organisations it is often the new girl or boy who questions why things are done the way they are done? Why is such and such a behaviour tolerated, and how can people work under such stress/disorganisation or micromanagement?

To the existing staff all of this seems normal, in fact they don't even notice, never mind question the status quo. They have become cognitive misers towards the subject, unwilling to devote anytime to thinking about such things.

A couple of years ago, when Miascape was still a very small company of two directors, a couple of temps and the occasional uni student who came to us in the holidays, we decided to recruit a third consultant.

We spent a lot of time training our approach to them, which they got. We spent lots of time going through the process of how we interacted with our clients, which they got. We spent time working through all the admin stuff which they totally got. Everything seemed great. We considered our new employee to have "fitted in".

However, a couple of months later it became apparent that this was not the case. Whereas the two directors seemed instinctively to know what was really important to this young, growing business, our third person didn't. It was almost as if they were working for a different organisation, they just shared an office with us. For example, as a small business sales and cash flow take precedence over anything else. Our third employee seemed to want to plan work and plan resource, we on the other hand just wanted to grow the business and saw no need for such plans.

Unfortunately we parted company and then started to think a bit harder about why it had gone so wrong.

The answer was fairly simple when we spent the time thinking more deeply. We had given our employee all the induction he needed apart from sharing our filters with him. The filters we had evolved over the first few years which made us, to a degree, ignore planning resource as we simply did not have the time to do such things faced with the more immediate task of bringing money in to pay everyone.

We had not taken the time to understand the unwritten rules by which we worked, the "givens". We had not tested these unwritten rules were valid and we had certainly not communicated these rules to our employee. We had not inducted them into our culture!

Filtering, as we call it, is the ability to attenuate information. It is important because it allows us to ignore unimportant noise. I use noise in the widest sense meaning noise in all the senses (touch, taste, sound, sight, smell) Imagine you arrive at work one morning and a pneumatic drill has set up camp outside your office. To begin with you can hardly hear yourself think. The drill owner reliably informs you that it will only take six weeks to complete the project. Groan, you pop two paracetamol and try to get on with your work.

Several weeks pass and a colleague comes to meet you in your office. "how on earth do you cope with this noise?" he says. "What noise" is your likely response. The chances are that by this point you have filtered the noise as a "given", something in which there is no point in you giving any of your attention to.

So being a cognitive miser has its ups and it's downs but the point here is to be able to acknowledge our filters and to decide if we are filtering the right stuff. Have we challenged our own thinking recently? Or have we just applied the same thinking to a similar situation because, on the face of it, it is a bit of a "given"?

Many people in business have gone through years of academic training, studying every aspect of work, but it is practically a given that they have never been taught how to think harder. They will have been exposed to the work of all the "best thinkers" in the world of business, and will have learned how to understand and rehash other people's ideas, using their words and a preordained vocabulary. Strikingly absent will be the tools necessary for better, harder, more refined, original thought.

This is where Miascape's models and methods come in, because our focus is not on telling people what to think, but on helping them learn how to think better, delving deeper into their own and others' reservoirs of intellect, knowledge and ability. Real breakthroughs come when we exhaust the thinking strategies that we have grown used to employing; when we have to break through everything we think we know to reach a new level of understanding and insight. We also need to learn how to ask those who work with us and for us to use their own thinking strategies and to express their own opinions, so that the organisation benefits from the insights of all of its members, not just senior management.

How can we learn how to think harder? Try the following exercise you will need paper pen and a stopwatch/timer;

Take 30 seconds to list ten girls' names.

Finished? How did that feel? Fairly easy I guess.

Now give me another twenty girls names (different to the last list) you have 40 seconds.

How did that go? A little more difficult but still easy?

OK finally, give me another 30 girls names. You have one minute to do this.

So what happened?

The first ten names were easy. You probably felt that your mind worked faster than your writing hand. You possibly used a strategy of "Girls I know" or, if you are in the office right now "Who do I work with?"

The second ten girls' names are a bit harder. Perhaps you stopped to think a little during this. It still didn't challenge your mind too much. Chances are you moved onto new strategies "my girlfriend's names" or "final year at school girls". Perhaps you found yourself using association e.g. " my Gran had a friend with a really unusual name, I can remember her perfume but not her name, my friend's dog had the same name, Gertrude that was it!"

The thing about this is you are using recall, memory!

When I asked you for the final 30 , I am sure many of you just stopped, it was just too much trouble to do this for the sake of some book! For those of you who did join in you probably groaned as you went about your task. As humans we do not like thinking harder, especially when we see no immediate benefit to it. Why didn't the first few girls names do?

When you tried to come up with names however, I guess they were more creative, on the whole, than your first ten. Your original strategies may have been abandoned in favour of awaiting blinding insight. You could probably feel yourself thinking harder, scratching your head, pushing yourself into just a bit more thinking. When was the last time you did this for a work topic?

Humans are cognitive misers! We have to push ourselves into

thinking harder. Now you have a sense of just how hard you can push your thinking, try doing this the next time you are asked for your ideas or thoughts at work. Try thinking harder and pushing yourself into that head scratching place.

In this exercise you probably heard the request as "give me some existing girls' names". Actually I asked you for "some girls' names".

Who was called apple before Gwyneth Paltrow used it? Who was ever called blanket?

When a request is made of us, it is human nature to reach for what we know or at least strategies which we know that will help us answer the request. We sometimes attenuate the question to what we think we have been asked and do not really pay much attention to the real question. It sounded like such a familiar question there was really no reason for you to attend to it at all. If however I had asked you to make up some words which we could entitle "Girls Names for the Next Millennium" that is certainly a different question which would have required a bit more thought into what you being asked to do.

Rarely will we think so hard that we cast aside existing strategies (in the case of this exercise it was using recall through a variety of prompts) and use something else (e.g. Zenthya which I made up because I like the sounds these letters make).

You have just experienced thinking harder. If you can recognise this in yourself and you can push and prod yourself into a place where you will drop existing strategies, then you really have the art of thinking harder. Some people are more naturally inclined towards this than others but we can all improve, and, I believe, we can all push our thinking that bit further.

How else can we improve our thinking as a typical human cognitive miser? Another exercise I hear you groan, try being a client of ours!

Try this; let your thoughts just run. Do not try to take them in a direction just let them go. You probably find yourself in some sort of narrative and the thoughts are about events or things which connect in some way or another, possibly linked through events, time or people.

Now try thinking only in pictures. Allow your mind to flash up as many pictures as it can without trying to connect or comment on them. If you start trying to hone your thoughts, notice this and try to go back to letting things run.

Thinking in pictures frees our minds up to do different things. If someone asks you where your organisation will be in 12 months try to think about the future in pictures and then capture it in more structured thought, words and statements.

This is why approaches such as mind mapping have been so successful in memory but we can also use this technique to free up thinking.

You may have your own ways of freeing your thinking up. In our experience however very few people apply this to every request which is made of them.

So in order to think harder we need to free our thinking up sometime to "unstick" it, we need to think harder to head scratching point and we need to be aware of the filters which influence how we think about things. These filters can be part of the environment in which we work, so if in doubt, find the nearest new person and ask them for 40 girls' names.

11

Changing Mental Models

Next to React, Reframe, Align and Embed, the story of mental models and changing mental models is probably the next most crucial element of smart transformation!

In previous chapters we have mentioned mental models and how they can be helpful to us and, at times, not so helpful. In order to effect *Reframe* in a transformation, we need to dig deeper into what we mean by mental models and then work out what it means to change mental models. Finally we will discuss what can be achieved following a shift in our mental models. What does it free us up to do?

Let us begin by talking about the stuff we cannot change. Our personality is partly innate (we are born with it, i.e. *nature*) and partly gained from how we are brought up (*nurtured*). In psychology there has been much debate over which is dominant or exclusive. This debate is likely to go on for some time to come. We tend to accept that it is a bit of both but that, probably, nurture has the greatest impact. However, I heard on the radio recently that there is a gene which predisposes people to eating garlic!

So in talking about mental models we are not talking about our basic personality type. It is more about how this basic personality, over the years of its life, has experienced the world and learned from each experience. Following each experience the learning has been stored somewhere as a "this is what happens when..." model. This is combined with the emotions which this event has brought about, the outcome and what strategies helped us to get through it. If the strategies worked once then they are bound to work again, right?

As we have mentioned before, on most occasions mental models are very helpful. They are based on our experience, both things which we have been personally involved in and those events where we have learned from what someone else has experienced, by observation.

For example, as a child you may have touched a fire and learnt very quickly that fires are hot. However you may have learnt this lesson indirectly as your older brother may have spared you some pain by touching the fire before you and crying. You would be unlikely to go and try touching the fire for yourself. A mental model about engaging with fire is now born. This is a really helpful mental model to have about fire as a five-year-old and you didn't even have to suffer to learn that potentially painful lesson.

We can also build mental models up by what other people, for example our parents, tell us. If your parents told you "never, ever, ever go near that fire *or* you will be burnt and you will have to go to hospital," and you were of an age to be able to understand the language, it is highly unlikely that you would go near the fire. You would have sufficient confidence in your parents' judgement that you would not be inclined to test the theory out for yourself.

So mental models are built up from what we experience and accept as true and what we are told by people who we trust and rely on. Interestingly this is also a definition of belief. We believe things because we have experienced them or we are told by someone we trust and rely on. So mental models are life a belief set but involve unconscious and conscious filtering.

So how do these experiences grow as we do and what relevance do they have to change and transformation in organisations?

If as a very small child you had a bad experience with a dog, there is a chance that you are still very wary of dogs. Perhaps you even felt angry or aggressive towards the dog, so great was your own fear. Your strategy as a child was probably to put as much space between you and that dog as possible. This strategy seemed to work so you continue to employ it. Even if one hundred people have told you since that you have nothing to worry about, and there is really no need to cross the road to avoid the dog, it is unlikely that your wariness would disappear. Unless we actively worked on changing your mental models about dogs, your behaviour would stay the same, you would continue to cross the road. Psychologists, therapists and counsellors have known about, and been successfully treating behaviour like this for a long time.

If we were tackling the dog problem the same way most organisations try to get through transformation, by telling people to change, you can imagine the dialogue.

Organisation: *"Just touch the dog, it won't hurt, it will be great. It is so much more efficient than crossing the road all the time. You MUST learn to be Ok with the dog."*

Individual: *"No, I don't think so. Get lost, I resign!"*

Your mental model had been created from your early experience and the way in which you perceived that experience. Now here comes the hard part. Fundamentally, your perception of the dog experience and the successful strategies you employed cannot be wrong because it is your personal experience and it was perceived by you, with your eyes, ears, smell, taste and feel, and all of your experiences in your head up to that point in your life, so how can it be wrong? If I said "stop avoiding dogs" would you change your behaviour? Perhaps while I was around watching, but other than that I guess you would revert to type.

So how do we change mental models or at least refine them?

Let's go back to learning about fire as a child and your beliefs about dealing with fire.

Years later you decide to take part in a fire-eating course at a circus school. How easy is it to arrest your early-formed mental models? In order for you to even contemplate touching fire, something in the way you currently "think" about fire must change.

Imagine your instructor (who you see as an expert) gives you further knowledge about the nature of fire which shows you that your current thinking about it is inaccurate. For example he may tell you that some parts of flames are hotter than others and won't burn you if your hand is moving through reasonably quickly; that the moisture on your tongue acts as great insulation to the heat as the flaming torch is past over; that some fuels burn hotter than others; this is how this type of flame behaves and this is how to touch it safely. You may add all this new knowledge to your mental model which may now read "Fires can burn but not all flames are the same – however, it can still burn you."

Once you have gained the skills perhaps you can understand how people manage to eat fire without being burnt. Perhaps by testing your new thinking for yourself your mental models will be rewritten again. They may now read "If you learn how to work with fire you can touch it by employing certain skills and knowledge which will prevent you from being hurt."

You still recognise that fire can be dangerous; you have not thrown all caution to the wind. You have, however, changed the way you think about fire and as such your behaviour has been able to change to allow you to become an amateur fire-eater. I have to say at this point I have never eaten fire, nor do I have any knowledge on how to do so. If you are actually interested in becoming a fire-eater, I suggest you buy a book written by someone with more knowledge than me.

If I had told you "just eat the fire, you will be fine" what do you think your response would be? I am sure you would have declined my helpful suggestion in one way or another. I am fairly certain that I would be left in no doubt that you had no intention of eating the fire.

So why on earth do organisations speak to their staff like this about change!

How often have we experienced individuals in an organisation whose behaviour is typed as "inappropriate". Perhaps they appear aggressive or disengaged. Perhaps they simply refuse to do something. How often do we, as observers of such behaviour, question where it is coming from? Mostly we *react* to it, which in turn informs that individual that the environment does make them feel angry or disengaged.

Perhaps you have been this person. If not, then think about the following scenario, from a case study of a real client:

You are an individual in a large organisation. Following a particularly difficult year you are asked to attend a meeting where you, along with many others are told that the company is integrating several departments and it's going to be great. Several weeks later, amidst total chaos as to what everyone should be doing, your boss challenges you about your performance. He himself is clearly under immense pressure. You feel ill-equipped with skills and lacking the leadership you need in order to make the integration happen. Several more months go by and nothing changes except the demands of your boss. During your annual appraisal you are told your performance is below par and that you should consider looking for alternative employment.

With a new mortgage and small children to support it is a terrifying time. You do find another job in a great company and it's the best thing you have ever done. You have certainly experienced "integration".

Ten years later you manage your own department in your organisation. Following the economy slipping into recession you are asked to meet with the board. It is simple, the board tells you: in order to cut costs and survive this recession the answer is to integrate several departments. It will be great and the board are confident you are the best person to do it!

How would you feel in that moment? What thinking would be taking place? What emotions would you feel? What behaviour might we see if we were board members?

It is interesting that as board members we would have nothing to go on but your external behaviour.

We would have no knowledge of your mental models surrounding "integration". We would be unlikely to know the impact of your previous bad experience of integration. We would be clueless as to the emotion you felt at the prospect of heading up an "integration". We would simply expect you to see it through our eyes, as a great cost-saving exercise with you our treasured employee at the helm. What could possibly be problematic about that?

Thankfully we were asked to work with this individual and the department which they headed up. The individual in question was one of the most able leaders we have met, yet, without the opportunity and space to explore current thinking and challenge mental models, it is likely that the integration would have been a disaster and the individual a casualty of traditional change management.

It is clear that, on the whole, organisations have not grasped the concept of changing thinking rather than telling people to change their behaviours. Despite the success of the many therapists involved in curing thousands of people of phobias and bad habits (e.g. smoking and being scared of dogs) with cognitive therapy, the theory has not been transferred into managing people, until now!

Ask yourself the question, what stops transformation? What are the big blockers in making real change happen in organisations? We have asked hundreds, perhaps thousands, of people what they see the issue as. The answer is a resounding STAFF ENGAGEMENT! By staff engagement we mean everybody, from the CEO to the middle mangers to the new recruits to support staff. Staff engagement at any level can be and indeed is a problem.

OK, so we have a grasp of the concept of mental models, we can probably recognise a few in ourselves and others. It is clear that mental models (our thinking) drives our behaviours (and emotions) and we know from the evidence that this is the stuff which prevents transformation in organisations (also groups and individuals). So the question now must be "How do you change mental models? How do you transform thinking?"

At university I had a poster on my wall of the cartoon character Garfield. He had many books strapped to his arms and legs and the caption read "I'm learning by osmosis". I use to think how great it would be if this were indeed the case. Although I've never been able to recall anything from an unopened book, I have certainly learned things about life without really paying any conscious attention at all.

To us, and to many of the great psychologists including Albert Bandura, humans constantly learn and adapt depending upon the experiences we are exposed to. Sometimes we are not even aware that an experience has had any effect on us whatsoever. We perhaps were even unaware of the experience; we filtered it as it was not important. Filtering, however, does not mean that it is not in our brain somewhere! It just means that it did not hit conscious thought.

If we start to talk about behaviour, describing the behaviour of both ourselves and those around us, we can start to reverse engineer what thinking may be governing these behaviours. It is not straightforward, but by taking the time to actually examine what we think, what others think, without critique, then we create an opportunity for thinking to change. However, something must destabilise our existing beliefs. It is not enough to merely point them out. We need to be compelled by something.

Often what we believe is not reflected in our behaviour. When this is pointed out to us it feels uncomfortable, so much so that we either have to change our behaviours or change our beliefs and values. This is called cognitive dissonance and was first discovered and studied by a guy called Festinger. The concept has been developed and used widely across many fields but not generally in the area of people transformation.

As an organisation we have been utilising Festinger's model of cognitive dissonance to transform the thinking of thousands of people who were tasked to "change" in some way by their organisation. Some of our projects have entailed working with hundreds of people over several sessions to integrate two parts of an organisation, at other times we have worked with the senior board members at the very beginning of an organisational transformation. It is completely scalable and can be applied anywhere.

For example, many of the people we work with talk about having too many meetings. However, when we examine their actions we can see that they are attending and organising lots of meetings. From this we suggest that their thinking must be that having lots of meetings is good. Usually we take a lot of flak as they shout back, "No we don't believe that at all!" At this point everyone feels a bit uncomfortable. It is clearly not that these people are not trying their best or working hard, but somewhere in their mental models there is a suggestion that meetings are good and achieve a lot. In reality this is rarely the case!

Something has to change. Most commonly it is the belief set

that is challenged and needs to be rewritten. In the case of "meetings" the new belief set commonly is rewritten along the lines of "the right type of meeting, with the right people and content, and the right length, is effective use of time, and I will reduce the number of meetings I hold."

Our clients have come up with fantastic insights which have literally halved their number of meetings overnight. If, however, we had strolled up and just told people to halve their meetings it simply would never have happened – or at least not without huge resentment which undoubtedly would have led to things slipping back to where they once were.

The power of working with thinking (mental models) rather than behaviours is that it brings about real, sustainable transformation in which the individual(s) have been engaged. No-one has told them what to do. What has taken place is an exploration of current thinking in light of the current challenge and an insight in the individuals (due to a feeling of cognitive dissonance) that their beliefs were actually not accurate and required some rewriting.

If all the individuals involved in a transformation have the opportunity to explore their thinking, what can we expect might happen next?

Going back to our $E=mc^2$, React-Reframe-Align-Embed, we have given these individuals the opportunity and space in which to reframe. However, rather than allow a natural reframe of the situation we destabilised the balance between thinking (mental models), the environment and behaviours (and emotions) by challenging current mental models. Insights were gained into existing thinking and mental models were rewritten leaving an opportunity for new emotions and behaviours to be.

This group begins to align as to where they are going and what that requires of them. They understand their part to play and are motivated by their own thinking not by someone constantly telling them what to do. The project is completed and no-one refers back to the old world and "if only we still did it that way". Transformation has reached. Embed!

Mental models and the part they have to play in real transformation of individuals, groups and organisations cannot be overestimated. They form the basis of both the written and unwritten rules of an organisation. In order to make transformation more probable we must first consider what existing mental models may prevent us from getting there and explore a new mental model we may wish to adopt.

12

The "So That" of Business

A surprising number of people don't know why they are working so hard. They don't know what they want.

We have a simple exercise that we use to help people think a lot harder about why and how they do the things they do that we refer to as the "so that" of business. Imagine an organisation that is working hard at coming up with job strategies and titles in order to complete a project. They decide they need a project manager. But why? So that everyone else will get their work done on time. Well, that's an answer, but it doesn't go very deep. Why does everyone need to get their work done on time? So that the project will be finished to their client's satisfaction. And why does that matter? So that the client will return to them and recommend them to others. Again, what's the big deal about that? So that the company will grow and prosper and hopefully expand into other markets. Now we're getting closer, but we can still dig deeper yet.

We once worked with an SME which is fairly unusual for us but it proved to be a very important session. We met with the senior directors, one of whom owned the company. They were great guys, passionate about what they did, about being the best in the market and about their staff. In fact the story they told us was really engaging and we got a sense that this was a company ready to transform.

After the preliminary chat we got down to work. The first thing we wanted to know about was the company vision, what message was being given to staff? What was it that they were being asked to deliver?

The directors told us that the vision was to achieve a turnover of £4 million the following year. Much to everyone's obvious surprise I asked, "Why?" The two directors looked at me blankly. "What do you mean why? Surely it's obvious?" "No, not really," I said. "Tell me your vision as if I were one of your top salespeople," I said. A similar statement was made to the first with little embellishment. I reflected the statement back with a simple question attached, "The vision is to turn over £4 million, so that?"

With that, the floodgates opened. Whenever the thinking dried up I asked "So that?" Soon the directors were joining in, enjoying thinking harder than they ever had about why they were doing what they were doing. They saw the value of thinking harder and began to challenge each other in the same way. It was truly fascinating and I appreciate now that the session was responsible for the "So that?" question which would be used to invigorate the thinking of many leaders to come.

Prior to our session the directors had thought little further than figures, which, as we know is not really a vision that everyone can buy into and become passionate about. They seemed to have jumped right into changing the behaviour of the existing sales force. This was being done mostly through company car choice and bonuses.

The company had approached us as they were surprised that although some of their staff were highly engaged and highly successful in sales, the rest were technically very good but seemed somewhat disengaged. With a recession approaching the plan was to cut those who were not performing but that would leave the company with a reduced technical ability. How could they get everyone engaged and performing?

To the senior management £4 million seemed like a pretty good vision; *they* could certainly buy into it. But in reality, a £4 million turnover was not their vision because when asked "so that?" a huge list followed. It was the first time this list had probably been thought about and certainly verbally aired. It included such things as "to grow and protect ourselves from the inevitable downturn, so that we can continue to make profit, so that our sales people can get better company cars, better training and access to professional exams, so that we retain the best sales people, so that we continue to thrive, so that we are in the strongest position possible on the other side of this recession..."

In this "So that?" list it is easy to see areas where most people could buy in and become engaged. In the previous vision of a £4 million turnover it was difficult to get excited about it if you were a salesperson without the emotional attachment to the company which the company owner inevitably has. It turned out that only half of their staff were motivated by company car speak, the rest had a vested interest in their career, the necessary professional exams and a feeling of job security.

Because they have rarely explored the "So that?" of the decisions they take, many organisations approach challenges the wrong way and undertake tasks in the wrong order.

On one occasion we worked with an organisation in the finance sector whose management team wanted it to become a learning organisation. The company had spent thousands on an online resource as well as a centre for excellence. In a specific tier of management there seemed to be a large discrepancy between individuals as far as learning went. The question which the company wanted to answer was, why was this the case? It was important for them to understand what was going on as these individuals were fairly crucial to succession planning.

We worked with the individuals involved and tried to

understand why the best were the best. It became evident fairly quickly that the best learners had never used either the online learning system nor had they set foot in the centre for excellence. How on earth were they learning and developing so rapidly? The key was in these top performers' network. Whenever they were faced with a new challenge or something they didn't know they simply turned to their extensive internal and external networks to find out how to tackle it. In reality what the organisation really needed was great networkers with an ability to ask for help – not necessarily great learners!

The outcome of this was that we went back and dug down further into the original thinking to find out the "So that?" of a learning organisation. The result was a U-turn on the learning facilities which were sidelined in favour of an "in depth" mentoring and coaching approach.

Understanding the real driving force behind work and business makes effort, work, meetings and decisions make sense – and when things do make sense, it's a lot easier to work practically toward solutions, thinking harder all the way.

As we discovered in an earlier chapter, humans are cognitive misers. We do as little thinking as we think is necessary to get us to where we want to go. We think to a depth and it is somewhat unnatural for us to go beyond this. It is also disconcerting if someone starts to talk at a much deeper level of thinking and has not taken us on the journey with them.

It is therefore important to make sure that once you have thought harder about why you are doing something, you tell those you need to engage the same story, step by step, from the beginning.

So how can you ensure you are getting to the "So that?" – and if you do, what difference will it make to your thinking?

Firstly, for goodness sake give yourself some time to think! It sounds like such an obvious statement, but consider the culture of your organisation for a moment. If you walked in one day and saw two members of your staff, one hard at work, tapping out emails furiously on the keyboard, and the other with hands clasped behind their head leaning back with eye shut, what would you think?

In some organisations we interact with, the behaviour of the emailing employee would be rewarded and that of the eyes-shut employee would be scorned. If you find yourself in this environment then how do you do your thinking? Is it the cultural norm to do thinking lying in bed at night and not on company time?

We have also worked with some companies where thinking is actively promoted. In these organisations resource has been put behind creating a culture where everyone has the time and the right to think about what they are doing. Less time is devoted to the traditional agenda-bound meeting and have instead been replaced by "So that?" meetings and otherwise Information-only meetings, called a chicken feed in one organisation, as nobody sits down – the person with the information simply feeds it to everyone and the meeting is then over.

Once an organisation gives authority to its staff to think harder, amazing things follow! Our experience is that these organisations have a culture of calm, creativity, originality and agility. They have by far the most engaged staff.

In one of these organisation, when you turn up at reception you are greeted by everyone in the same way. Let me explain a little. During one visit I was shown round the building and introduced to probably about 20 people. The interesting thing was that you could easily believe that each person could be the company owner or MD. They all had such enthusiasm and passion and were able to talk to me openly about their role and where they thought the company should go next without referring upwards.

I was being taken round by a friend of mine who happened to be the MD. At one point we walked into an area to chat to a technical guy. He was clearly thinking, drawing on a large white board and "in the flow". We stopped outside the door and my friend suggested that we came back later as Joe was obviously busy thinking.

It struck me then that this was unusual. In most organisations where I've turned up for a day of observation my usually senior host seems to think that it's more important to introduce me to people, regardless of what they are doing, than it is to be cognisant of the fact that the people working, thinking and creating are working on the business. Now what could possibly be more important than that?

We don't recommend that everyone should spend every minute of every day looking as though they are either thinking or sleeping, of course, and that this behaviour will never be challenged. To some degree it is the opposite. It is to create a culture where people are challenged to think harder, regardless of where they sit in the organisational hierarchy.

So giving people time and space to think is incredibly important but is it realistic in the real world?

The best leaders we know come across as having all the time in the world. When you walk into their office time seems to be suspended and nothing is more important than them being truly present in the meeting.

Think of some famous businesspeople – Sir Richard Branson, Gerry Robinson who sorted the NHS and showed a lot of people who was boss, and James Khan from Dragon's Den. Think about how they might think in order for them to behave in the way they do. From watching them on screen you certainly get the impression that they do not take thinking time lightly. Often they can be heard talking about "thinking" whether it's their thinking, time to think or a different way to think. Rarely do they take a statement at its face value. Although the wording may not be "So that?" it is clear that they regularly challenge thinking, and from their external behaviour I would suggest that this is a very natural both internal and external process for them.

The worst leaders we meet, whose organisations are usually in chaos, are those who have time for nothing and nobody. They don't eat, sleep or think and they always double-book every meeting. (If this sounds like you, please see the back of this book where you can arrange to come and join us for a day!)

There seems to be a mental model within these people that in order to be seen as working hard you need to be moving at breakneck speed. Statements are made and decisions either taken or put to one side in an instant without really any thought to the consequences. Now I place no blame here. This is clearly learnt behaviour which has been created and moulded by the interplay between environments and mental models. In order to change this type of behaviour we need to examine both the thinking and the environment.

So how do you get to the "So that?" of business?

When you have settled your mind, ask yourself what you are trying to do. Capture each statement as it comes to you and then ask "So that?" until you get to such a point that your highest intention becomes clear and you cannot further your thinking with any more "So that?" questions. Make sure you push your thinking to this point. If you try this exercise right now, you can skip reading the next couple of paragraphs as the benefits of thinking harder in this way will already be clear to you.

By asking "So that?", you are challenging your deeper thinking, i.e. it's in your head, where else would it come from? But until you challenge yourself to think about it, you cannot fully comprehend your subconscious drivers and the real reasons why you are doing what you are doing.

This deeper intention will not come as a surprise to you but what may be surprising is that it is linked firmly to the activity which you have just been pondering.

If you do not know fully why you are doing something, how can you expect to succeed?

Now, of course you can choose whether or not to share this deeper thinking with others. It may remain for your information only, for all sorts of reasons, or it may be widely shareable. If you are CEO of a company and your plan is to retire next year with the best pension you can get, then you may not want to headline all of your "So that?" thinking to your staff.

If you are a member of middle management and want to make as much bonus as you can this year to fund your mature graduate course next year, then you may not want to divulge your thoughts to the CEO of your highest intention which is driving your strategy this year. However, I suggest you think deeply about engaging him in your plans; sometimes people will support you even if they have little to gain from the outcome.

However, if you are planning to stay, then whatever your management position, you have a choice to make. You can *choose* how you wish to shape or influence the thinking culture of your organisation (or at least a part of that organisation), which in turn will govern the behavioural and emotional culture of your organisation which is what really impacts your bottom line. It's up to you to become a "So that?" organisation and to become a leader who also expects his staff to ask him "So that?"...

13

Space to Change Your Mind

This could be the shortest chapter in this book. It might be the longest one. No it might be the shortest, but then again it could be the longest. I am guessing that you are reading this and saying, "For goodness sake, make up your mind." The publisher told me to write a long chapter, so here goes.

In fact, most of our life is spent making up our minds. We make decisions about what we wear in the morning, what we eat for breakfast. Whether we speak to the person behind the counter in the paper-shop and whether the receptionist at work, assuming it's not you, gets a cheery hello. We decide if we get a coffee before we take our coat off or after we have spoken with our colleagues who are already in the office. Are you getting the picture? We constantly make decisions. Now these decisions are sometimes easy and sometimes complex. They exist on a continuum of easiness. Decisions are mental things and the language we use around them relates to a state of mind. "She decided to wear a red dress." Physically, in our world, we see her wearing a red dress, but if pushed we know that *in her head* she had a thought to wear a red dress.

Now if I changed the language and said we take *positions* on things, that feels different. We take positions on global warming, vegetarianism, slavery, domestic abuse, government policy, car designs, football teams, artists, designers, supermarkets and music. There is a physical element to the word "position". It conjures up in my mind at least a physical movement to a space. Taking a *position* on something makes me think of individuals moving towards a group of like-minded people.

I like to think of this movement in a physical sense. Imagine a pool table with indents in the surface the size of small saucers. If you throw the pool balls on the table they will bounce around until they find a home in one of the saucers. They come to rest in the pool craters and there they will stay. They have taken a position. The physical metaphor works well. In order to get the ball out of the crater, energy has to be expended to "get the ball rolling". By providing energy – that is, time, money, resources – we can move out of these metaphorical craters and move to a new one once we are over the lip.

Now I bet you are thinking that I am going to say "and just like people, if you give them a shove they will change their position." Well, I am not.

If you remember, the central theme of this book is that transformation in organisations occurs not when you change behaviour but when thinking transforms. Giving people a shove to change positions is easy and generally they will comply but they will constantly be looking back at the old crater with affection.

We have often thought that we should write a book on child management techniques as we have observed that most of the strategies we adopt to manage our children can be equally well applied to the adults we meet in organisations. That is not to say that the adults we meet are childish, just that the strategies we adopt are extremely similar.

Imagine a child that has been rebuked for some behavioural transgression. After crying they may withdraw into a sulk, become quiet and not want to engage in the activities of their peers even though that activity looks like fun. The more we tell them to "get involved" the more they refuse to do so. The strategy to adopt in that case is the following, and I am going to be long-winded here.

- *You know that you have broken a rule.*
- *You know that you are upset about being corrected.*
- *I know that you may feel embarrassed by your behaviour.*
- *I know that you can see these other children having a good time.*
- *What I am going to do to is give you space to change your mind.*
- *It is OK to stop the behaviour you are exhibiting and change your decision and join in if you wish.*
- *No-one will refer to the previous incident or behaviour.*
- *I am going to leave you to reflect on what I have said.*

Well in my experience, and I have quite a lot where children are concerned, at this stage the child will change their mind and join in. The sure-fire way of elongating the period of sulking is not to have the "space to change your mind conversation". To constantly tell the child to "stop being a spoil sport, get involved" just seems to deepen their resolve to stay in the sulk.

In our experience in organisations, and from what we have observed working with organisations this ability to give people the "space to change their minds" is sadly lacking. People in organisations become labelled as "difficult", "negative", "irritating", "boring", "entrenched", "old fashioned", "sarcastic", "unsupportive" and any other unflattering word you can think of.

Now I am going to digress a little here. We have worked with organisations that are anxious to give labels to their staff. The latest round of labelling that we have come across is to define people in terms of their strengths. However there have been many such labelling approaches that end up with people sharing their defined characteristics with their colleagues. I have not yet seen on a business card,

James Henderson,
Managing Director,
I am a wow person and
if I were a sandwich
I'd be salmon and cream cheese on brown
08700421340
07720076043

but I bet it will come. It seems that organisational development people (I&R) want to label people so that they can talk about them in an abstract way and build a development plan for the labels they don't yet have. "John you are too red, you need to have more blue and the squirrel is rising as the orange conflicts with the apple." What bollocks.

There is ample evidence in the literature that people *become* more like the labels that you give them. Start by googling Bertram R Forer's work on personality tests and follow the links. If you tell someone they are organised they become *more* organised. If you tell people they are *amusing* they (try to) become more amusing. If you tell someone they are the life and soul of the party that is how they will show up. Labelling people is dangerous. They become the label that you give them. The caveat to this is that they have to believe in what you are telling them. Now when these surveys are done they are subtly reinforced before, during and after. "This cost the organisation £250,000, it is going to make a difference." "The top 100 companies in the UK use this approach." "Richard Bigcheese uses this and swears by it." People begin to believe in these things and then adopt them and then become them. Belief happens in two ways. First if we experience something for ourselves and secondly if someone we trust the person who tells us it is true. Imagine you are in an organisation and someone tells you that you are going to be assessed and given a label which can be used to tell people what you are. The journey has started, this sounds good... so you become a *Begonia* to Sharon's *Daisy*. Fantastic.

Guess what? You immediately investigate "Begonia" and unconsciously or consciously become more begonia-like. Sharon is becoming more "Daisy". If you do not believe me try this exercise. The next time you are with a friend tell them that when you have conversations with them you always go away feeling better as they always say something funny to lighten your day. Repeat it in the conversation a couple of times. Now monitor your conversations going forward. The incidence of "funny" will increase. I do this all the time to people. Another one to try is to tell them they "always approach me with a smile". This one works too. As you get more adept at slipping these into conversations, mention that "your ability to mimic a parakeet in the middle of a sentence always astounds me." No I am joking here but you can see where I am going, I hope.

To summarise. People become what you tell them they are. So if you continue to point out to them behaviour which they once adopted, the chances are they will demonstrate that behaviour more not less often.

Back to the shortest chapter, or is it the longest?

Our observation in organisations is that not only do people get labelled by "official" processes; they also get labelled unofficially in the work place. Let's start with the simple. Carol is a Manchester United supporter. Colin is a coffee drinker. Charlotte never touches cheese. Let's move to the less simple. Sophie is a planner, Lucy is an innovator and Laura is an academic. Tom constantly challenges. Now let's move to the downright dangerous. Matthew is negative. Dorothy is a blocker and Terry is obstinate. Remember, people become more of what you give them a label to be.

So we all know who the difficult characters are in the organisation, or the team or the monthly board meeting. I bet you can name three of them right now. Not only that – believe me, they will know who they are too. At one point the exhibited behaviour, when reflected back, may have embarrassed the individual, but trust me after twenty years of Liz being labelled as the most scary senior manager in the organisation, do you really think that Liz doesn't live up to that, just a little bit?

So by labelling these people as difficult or entrenched they are likely to become more difficult and entrenched. It is a simple concept isn't it and one that needs to be addressed. So what can you do? Give them space to change their mind.

If you need to give someone space to change their minds there are many ways you can do this. The most simple and effective is to tell them. This is best done through a formal coaching session. "Jim, you probably know *(they will)* that the team regards you as difficult to work with and entrenched in your views about the project. I want to give you *the space to change your mind.* When you leave my office today, you have a choice. You can carry on as you are or you can make a conscious decision to be different. Here is the opportunity and space for you to change your mind." You will be surprised how effective this is an transforming individuals.

So let me put this in simple terms. If I have been a lifelong supporter of Manchester United but I now live in Scotland and all my colleagues and friends have been pointing out that really I should take up a Scottish team to support. How much easier would that be if all my pals in Manchester said, "Hey Duncan, I guess now you are in Scotland it's time to support a Scottish team. We've decided it's cool if you want to transfer your allegiance to Queen of the South. No problems. We are giving you *the space to change our mind.*" Also, my Scottish friends don't all

Public Information

The Scottish Parliament
Pàrlamaid na h-Alba

If you have a question about the work
of the Parliament, please contact us:

✉ **Public Information Service**
The Scottish Parliament
Edinburgh EH99 1SP

☎ **Tel: 0800 092 7500** or
0131 348 5000
Fòn: 0131 348 5395 (Gàidhlig)
Textphone users: 0800 092 7100

📱 **Text: 07786 209 888**
You can also order a free leaflet
pack by text. Just text PACK
and your name and address.

@ **Email:**
sp.info@scottish.parliament.uk

www.scottish.parliament.uk

turn round and say "told you so" or "well I never" when I turn up to my first Queens of the South match; they welcome me and don't even draw attention to my new behaviour.

This book is full is obvious things, and this is one of them. If people are entrenched or labelled, in order for them to become something else you need to give them the space to change their mind.

So I guess it's a short chapter. But believe me it's an important one.

$$14$$

So How Do You Know You Are Thinking Harder?

We said right at the beginning that we would talk about what we found in organisations in relation to transformation and change. Throughout this book we have tried to illustrate what we found in an oblique way in order to give opportunities for insight. But let's just be explicit here for a moment. What we found was that management teams at all levels expected the physical change or the governance change to persuade people to change their minds. The thinking will follow the intention. This is not so. It is the thinking that *creates* the intention. We also found that changing behaviours dominates the agenda over changing thinking when in reality changing thinking changes behaviours until the thinking changes again. It is a truism. We found that managers and leaders in general have no time for the context of others, from the trivial "We won't stop until we find an answer (<silent> and I don't care if you have other commitments I am not aware of because you work for this company and I have first call on your time </silent>)" to the serious "This is what I have decided to do – what do you think? (<silent> and it better not be different to me</silent>)".

The change models that are being used are focused on

changing activity and behaviours, and transformation in the boardroom is attenuated to change on the shop floor. Amongst all this, though, we found beacons of hope. Individuals who were engaging, supportive, inclusive and still delivered. They were in a minority. Interestingly, the ones who got the "thinking harder" approach were the most challenging but immediately saw the relevance to what they themselves were trying to do without an underpinning structure. The "course tourists" never quite saw the benefits as the "thinking harder" approach came without an award, a workbook, a pen or a stress ball.

This book has been about transformation through thinking harder. We have not tried to be descriptive about the ten habits of highly effective transformers, but have tried to talk in a holistic way about key things that ensure transformation takes place. You may decide to "bolt on" this stuff as a "toolkit" that you use when you get in a spot – change your behaviours depending upon the environment you find yourself in. We will have been more successful if you absorb this stuff "by osmosis" and it becomes part of your new mental models. You will know when this happens when people comment on your new approaches in the workplace. One we often hear is "Jenny is so happy at the moment," or Jenny says, "You know I am enjoying what I do, I don't feel I need to find answers to everything and I realise there are things I don't know. Asking for help is not a weakness, it's a strength."

So for those of you who just skip to the end of the book to read the summary chapter in order to "bolt on" some skills, the furry dice approach as we call it, or those of you who "buy the gear but have no idea" here is a summary of some of the main points we make in the book. However, if you don't understand the context in which they are made you will be standing on the grass with your thousand-pound driver in your hands and look down to find you are playing rugby not golf.

So how do you recognise in yourself and others that you are

"thinking harder" on our terms?

Stop thinking about action and start thinking about reaction.
Talking actions is easy. We do it without thinking. I am typing this book now without a thought of the actions taken to press the key on my old laptop. Taking actions is automatic. What is more important is for me to think about the reaction that these words will have on you and try to expand the paragraph to ensure you come with me on this word journey. Similarly in transformation, thinking about the reaction that will happen given any set of circumstance is thinking harder. Here is a real case. "We are going to move to Swindon from London, you will be compensated financially and everyone will have a role." Excellent. This totally excludes the context people find themselves in and assumes that by offering financial reward everyone will be on board. Not true. Explore the reaction fearlessly; it will ease the journey.

Never assume your current thinking strategies are appropriate for your current problems.
Have you ever played the game where you are asked a series of questions in succession and you have to give the answer to the first question when you are asked the second question, and the answer to the second question when you are asked the third question and so on? Not only is it ludicrously hard as your brain fights the natural desire to give the correct answer to the correct question, the answers sound bizarre and often funny to the audience. Let's try it.

Q1. Who was the leader of Social Democratic Party in Germany during the Second World War? – No answer.

Q2. What is known as the Old Man of the Jungle? – Adolf Hitler.

Q3. What drink is made from fruit juice and coconut? Orang-Utan.

Q4. Which female gymnast was the first to get perfect 10s on the floor exercise? Pina Colada.

And so on. The strange thing is that our friend from planet Zog would consider the answers to be completely plausible as they *sound* right. They are answers that have been right before, and sound plausible in the next question, but are not right. The analogy I am drawing here is that previous strategies are unlikely to be appropriate for situations we have not seen before even though they may feel right. The "thinking harder" approach advocates not using your existing thinking strategies to solve new problems. You will know when you are thinking harder when you hear groups of people destroying the previous ways of doing things and creatively developing new strategies.

*Listen to the language of others, speak in the language of others and then introduce **your** language slowly and start to use **your** language.*

Language is personal. Begin to listen to the language that individuals use. Begin to listen to the language groups use. Begin to listen to the language that organisations use. Use that language back to them. I know of a large organisation that plays a game on suppliers and colleagues. They introduce a phrase into their vocabulary and they score a point if they hear it used back. The person who told me this said that they had scored a point by introducing the phrase "swallow the frog" meaning "dealing with a difficult issue" – i.e. "We will have to swallow the frog on that one." Sure enough, in a telephone conversation some time later a supplier was heard to utter the phrase, "We'll swallow the frog on that one." One point. People are hugely susceptible to language. Whilst I don't advocate playing games like this, the principle is right. If people use "change" instead of "transformation" don't correct them; use "change" for a while, and then introduce "transformation" giving a definition of the difference as you do. Pretty soon people will start using "transformation" not "change". If you are thinking harder you are listening to the message not the words that are used. We can use our child analogy here. If a child is telling you a story and they use the wrong tense or say "sheeps" instead of "sheep" and you correct them in the story, pretty soon they will stop telling you stories. We are just the same when adults. "Whom" or "who" does matter at some point but not when you are listening to a story. Not only does correction derail their thinking; it derails yours too.

Involve the nay-sayers.
The people who say it can't be done usually have good reason to say so. Generally it is because they can see, feel or even *be* something that they think you have missed. When you are in the "thinking harder" mode you involve the nay-sayers as a positive input to your team. Excluding the nay-sayers prevents you from being challenged. You are not afraid of that are you? Use their energy to tell how it would work if you could get it to work. Generally it just needs a gentle "thinking harder" approach to get these people engaged.

Talk transformation not change.
Distinction is key. Once you can speak with distinction your messages become clear. Those people who know their subjects become authoritative on distinction. For example you see a motorbike, while I see a three-cylinder, single swing arm Triumph, probably 2003 vintage. I see a bridle on a horse, you see

a Weymouth Bridle used for showing or dressage. We get more accuracy the greater distinction we have. So let's be distinct. "Thinking harder" advocates a transformational approach not a change approach. If you don't have that distinction you are going to have to read the chapter on "Baking the cake" rather than just look for the quick fix in this chapter.

Acknowledge the "thinking harder" state in yourself and others.
If we fundamentally agree that in transformation people go through four stages – React, Reframe, Align and Embed – it is extremely useful to know what stage we are in or our colleagues are in for any particular set of circumstances. It is no good having an *Embed* conversation with someone who is still *reacting*. I recently rang up a client to chase an unpaid invoice. I got through to the CEO's PA expecting to have a conversation about a tardy payment. I asked how she was as a precursor to the conversation and she replied that she had heard that morning that the CEO had resigned from his position and the PA's role was up in the air. The PA was in *React* mode. There was no way she was in a position to have a conversation about my issues when her world was in turmoil. I made a weak excuse and came off the phone without discussing my issue. Two days later I called back and the conversation I wanted was possible. Using the intelligence we have to judge where people are in the React-Reframe-Align-Embed continuum can help us determine appropriate responses. "Thinking harder" people always know where they and others are.

Explore beyond your immediate knowledge.
When faced with a problem we apply the strategies and knowledge we already have to deal with it. How often do we think "What do I need to find out about to deal with this issue?" We deal with the issue in real time. The "thinking harder"

approach advocates thinking about what it is you don't know, and what you need to find out about before attempting a solution. Of course, if there is an incoming bomb we do not recommend contemplating action for too long. This approach is best applied when there is thinking time available. How often can we find time to put things right when they go wrong but can never find the time to do some thinking up front? Look at problems through fresh eyes and don't let the first idea on the table dominate the conversation. It is a proven fact that first ideas in conversation dominate thinking and prevent creative solutions. Once all the ideas are on the table, ask: "So if we couldn't use any of these ideas what would we do?" Now you are thinking harder and life gets creative.

Transform your questions to look backward from the future.
Think of the scenario. You have announced a transformation and you ask for feedback. The response you get is a list of things that are going to prevent you from doing it. You are already off on the wrong foot asking people to identify a whole host of barriers to completion. It's a natural approach and a natural response. If you are taking a "thinking harder" approach, ask the question in this way: "If we were in a place where we had completed this transformation what would we have had to do to get here?" You get all the same barriers identified but described in positive rather than negative terms and an engaged staff in their delivery.

Realise that the decision you make can be modified downstream.
We all consider our decisions to be the right decisions at the time we make them. But we know that good decisions can have bad outcomes and bad decisions can have good outcomes. Adopting the "thinking harder" approach means that you make decisions but acknowledge at the point that you make them that they can

be changed if they turn out to not be the right ones. The important thing here is, for goodness sake make the decision! But don't forget that if you don't think harder and you develop a *culture* of changing decisions, that will negatively impact your bottom line.

Transformational organisations engage in decision-making. It is better referred to as direction setting. You decide to move in one direction because the indicators tell you to do that, but have the flexibility and skills to deal with the complexity and risk such that your organisation is not surprised if that decision is changed. Do not assume that every decision is so important that you can't move in a different direction later. It sounds simple but it makes decision-making easier if you know it can be changed downstream.

Accept decisions are made on attenuated data and decisions can, if necessary, override emotive (non-substantive) objections.
No-one has all the facts. We have to make decisions at some point. We have to make decisions on attenuated data. But that is OK. If you are thinking harder you will realise that no business decision can be made with all the facts. The world is too complex. Don't speak in absolutes as you do not have exhaustive data. Learn to distinguish between emotive objections and substantive objections. You can make decisions if objections are emotive, but not when there are substantive objections. What is the difference? If I offer to take you in my car to Exeter and tell you I have a ten year old Discovery and you say you wouldn't be seen dead in a car less than two years old, then that's emotive. If you tell me you observe that my engine has just dropped on the floor then that's substantive.

Involve those that know.

If you adopt a "thinking harder" approach you involve those who have the knowledge. Make it your job to discover who knows what and match your requirements to those who have the knowledge. Do not assume seniority means more knowledge. Seniority leads to attenuation and smoothing of success and failures. Involve those who know.

Make time available up front rather than downstream.

"I can give you five minutes in between flights to Cairo and Delhi if you can catch me," or "We can never get the management team together more than once a month, a whole day to discuss this is out of the question." How many times have we heard this type of thing? When you are thinking harder you are asking yourself, "If we don't get this right what are the consequences and what time would I have to throw at it then to resolve the issue?" People who think harder don't just think in the "now"; they think in the "then" and make resource allocations with the "then" in mind.

Transform yourself first.

The world, the country, the county, the town, the village. The Organisation, the Division, the Department, the Group, the Team, the Office. What do they have in common? They are all populated by people. If you want to transform any of them start with yourself. The people we meet tend to talk about others but rarely look at themselves. Too many meetings? Reduce the ones you instigate. You want the organisation to listen? You start listening. You want to be quality driven? What's your quality like? You want people to deal with the big issues first, do you? Deal with your big issues first. We have met a number of managers who want to be "heard" by their staff, but have no time to listen to anyone else.

The "thinking harder" approach advocates transforming yourself first. Become the epitome of what you want others to be.

Consider whether or not you value someone's opinion before you react to what they are saying.
People who take the "thinking harder" approach know that we only *react* to events and people because we have an emotional reaction to them. Those who are not in the "thinking harder" mode tend to react according to the situation not to the people involved. This means that we are unduly expending emotional energy on things that should not be impacting us. If a random person stops you in the street and tells you that the way you are dressed is awful, how will you react? If your partner tells you the way you are dressed looks awful, how will you react? Have you ever considered asking this question before you react: "How much do I value this person's opinion?" If someone is aggressively challenging you in the workplace, ask the same question. Not only does it give you time to collect your thoughts; it helps you recognise whether the emotional energy you are expending is appropriate.

Give people space to change their mind
Remember the chapter in which I was confused about its length? If you have just skipped to here, you won't. Essentially, it is far easier for someone to transform their views if you give them the space to do so. If you are thinking harder, you recognise this fact. Encourage others to do this too. Make it a culture in your organisation. Barriers will be removed.

Statements made about others reflect your mental models.
You cannot NOT communicate what you are thinking. Making statements about others actually informs them and your colleagues or friends about how you think. "Janet is always late for meetings"

actually informs us that you think being on time for meetings is important. "Colin is not committed to this project" infers that the project can only be done with *commitment*. Given that context plays a part in statements we can gather an awful lot about what people think by what they say about others. "Do you think that red really goes with those shoes?" *(...because I clearly don't.)*

Be prepared not to fit in.
Thinking harder is hard. Working at this enlightened level is not easy. Be prepared not to fit in. Be evangelical but not smug. Educate others by example not by being directive. Be distinct.

Ask yourself and others "So that?"
Decisions have consequences. The future is determined by the decisions we take. By asking "So that?" we explore the future and explore the potential outcomes of our decisions. The "So that?" question explores the outcome you are trying to achieve at a level determined by you. It enables you to truly understand the reasons behind your actions. If you ask yourself the "So that?" question at least five times your level of understanding of your actions and decisions will be far in excess of your normal thinking process and will inform and engage the staff/people you involve.

Learn to take filters off.
Recognising that we look through the world through a personal set of filters is a powerful insight. Knowing what those filters are is even more powerful. Organisations that think harder learn to take the filters off so that they can look at things as if for the first time. Looking at the actions you are taking in light of the outcomes you require helps you reverse engineer the filters you are wearing. Thinking harder demands an ability to recognise and remove those filters.

Understand the unwritten rules.

The world is not run by written rules unless you transgress. The world runs on unwritten rules. Find out in your organisation what the unwritten rules are and ensure they are working in favour of transformation. In business the unwritten rule is that you can win any argument by saying, "But we put the customer first." Well actually you don't if you remain in the models of yesterday, stop intelligent conversations, label individuals and think superficially about issues.

Define words before you blow people away with hyperbole.

The strategic imperative. The encompassing governing framework. The excelling organisation. These have little impact on us as we have heard them so many times. They have become weak. The next time we hear them they will probably be "the intense strategic imperative", "the overarching compliance management system", "the hyper-organisation". As we overuse words we have to increase the intensity of the adjectives. What about just defining "organisation" to your staff? What about defining "compliance"? What about defining "strategy"? Define the simple words first and then excel in these. Service organisations are now speaking "lean" and six sigma. Ask anyone who talks about six sigma what one sigma is. The silence that follows...

Avoid speaking in absolutes.

People who think harder do not speak in absolutes. Listen to people around you. Who speaks in absolutes? Those people who are directive, overbearing and generally annoying. What do we mean? "You must do this." "This is the best restaurant ever." "You will enjoy this." "I have a better idea." "This is the way to do it." "No, this will work.". The absolute nature of these statements indicates to others that you consider yourself to be the arbiter of what is and what isn't. What about "This is a great restaurant", "There is another possibility you may enjoy this", "I have another idea", "Could we do it this way?", "This may work"? It's just language, I know, but the difference is it is engaging not disengaging.

Thinking is not necessarily linear.
Animals in the wild adopt an interesting strategy when looking for something. Observe a dog for instance sniffing to pick up a scent. They first of all pick a spot and move around that spot as a point of focus to pick up a scent. They explore a rough circle around the focal point and if they don't find what they want they do not move linearly and repeat the exercise, they leap to a completely different place. Learn to let your thinking do this. Don't just drill down ideas. Jump about. Be conscious of the fact that, as mentioned above, first ideas on the table dominate discussions.

Thinking time in conversations is acceptable.
Your brain cannot infinitely multi-task. There is a limit to what can be achieved when you are using all your input sensors and all your output devices simultaneously. Listening speaking and thinking at the same time is hard. Develop a strategy for fitting the thinking time in. Try not to overlap the thinking with the listening or the speaking. What seems like a long time to you when you pause to think will be hardly noticeable to others. Three seconds of thinking enhances conversational skills.

Think about the problem, then the process then the problem.
Thinking harder means getting the right process to solve the right problem. We are not talking about chemical synthesis or Fermat's Last Theorem here, we are talking about making sure that you

actually consider the management process for helping you and your teams deal with issues. Define the problem, organise a meeting, have an agenda, chat about it and then have an action plan. WRONG! That way you will use your existing thinking strategies to solve the problem. Define the problem, define the process by which you are going to try and explore the issue, communicate the problem and the process to your team and then try to solve it. Problem, Process, Problem, Solution.

The leader does not have all the answers.
People who think harder know that they cannot possibly have all the answers. However this does not stop people thinking that their ability in one field gives them the right to spout with authority in another. Seniority does not give you the power to have all the right answers. As a leader do not assume you have the best solutions and best ideas. Our experience has shown us that individuals who are highly qualified but have little management experience assume that management is easy and just common-sense. They think that people management is not something you have to learn about; anyone can do it. We know that is wrong. When you are thinking harder, explore who may have the relevant knowledge in your team. You might be surprised. Many years ago we worked with a client whose security guard on the entrance gate of the factory ran a £1m turnover business in her spare time. I only found that out when I chatted to her on a slow day.

Ensure people understand that you will listen to them extensively but you have decisions to make and they may not like the outcome.
A huge part of working with people in a "thinking harder" group is to manage expectations. Clearly indicate those things that they can influence and clearly indicate those things that they cannot.

However, still listen to their concerns on the issues in general. Make it clear that you have to make a decision in spite of objections you might hear, and clearly inform them of the difference between emotive and substantive issues. Working with a large group once we asked if we were ready to make a decision on an integration issue. The response was that there were too many objections to take the meeting to a conclusion. We explained the difference between emotive and substantive objections. We went round the room again and asked people to consider whether their objection was emotive or substantive. They were ALL emotive. We made a decision.

Staff engagement is not about getting people to say how good you or the organisation is.
Staff engagement is about their involvement in the company. It is not about saying how good the company is. Staff can be engaged in a poor company. People who think harder understand this.

So that is the essence of the "thinking harder" approach. By now you may be experiencing something called *Hindsight Bias* –that is, your view of where you have come from before you read this book will be skewed by the information in this book. You will think you already knew some of the things in this book and that it is so simple that you could not possibly not have known this stuff. Our answer to that is that you probably did know the majority of this stuff but, a bit like the ticking clock, until someone draws your attention to it you forget that it is there. Our other response is, of course, if you already know all the stuff in this book ask yourself if you are applying it.

It is our goal that you should never need another change consultant, but that you will create your own revolution by adopting a transformational approach in your own organisation. It is also our goal that organisations should be measured, not just on their turnover or bottom line, but on the real stuff: people, emotions and thinking.

So we come to the end of our adventure into the world of organisational transformation, but as you know there is no end nor a beginning. Change is constant; requests for transformation are always just around the corner. We hope that your response to this realisation is "bring it on!"

We look forward to meeting some of you in your new world in the future.

Index

Duncan Bury and Jane Buick are available for
seminars, after dinner speaking and corporate events.

If you would like to know more about the services Miascape offers,

One to One Coaching
Team Coaching
Board Coaching
Seminars
Transformation Skills
Transformation Architecture
Project Restart

please call our office in Edinburgh on:

08700421340

or email:

duncan@miascape.com
or
jane@miascape.com